RESUMES FOR
FORMER MILITARY
PERSONNEL

THIRD EDITION

RESUMES FOR
FORMER MILITARY PERSONNEL

With Sample Cover Letters

The Editors of McGraw-Hill

McGraw·Hill

New York   Chicago   San Francisco   Lisbon   London   Madrid   Mexico City
Milan   New Delhi   San Juan   Seoul   Singapore   Sydney   Toronto

The McGraw·Hill Companies

Library of Congress Cataloging-in-Publication Data

Resumes for former military personnel : with sample cover letters / the editors of McGraw-Hill.—3rd ed.
    p.   cm.
    ISBN 0-07-145881-6 (pbk. : alk. paper)
    1. Resumes—Employment.   2. Cover letters.   3. Veterans—Employment.
4. Retired military personnel—Employment.   I. McGraw-Hill Companies.

HF5383.R4374   2006
650.14′2—dc22   2005052233

1 2 3 4 5 6 7 8 9 0   VLP/VLP   0 9 8 7 6

ISBN 0-07-145881-6

McGraw-Hill books are available at special quantity discounts to use as premiums and sales promotions, or for use in corporate training programs. For more information, please write to the Director of Special Sales, Professional Publishing, McGraw-Hill, Two Penn Plaza, New York, NY 10121-2298. Or contact your local bookstore.

This book is printed on acid-free paper.

Contents

Introduction

Your resume is a piece of paper (or an electronic document) that serves to introduce you to the people who will eventually hire you. To write a thoughtful resume, you must thoroughly assess your personality, your accomplishments, and the skills you have acquired. The act of composing and submitting a resume also requires you to carefully consider the company or individual that might hire you. What are they looking for, and how can you meet their needs? This book shows you how to organize your personal information and experience into a concise and well-written resume so that your qualifications and potential as an employee will be understood easily and quickly by a complete stranger.

Writing the resume is just one step in what can be a daunting job-search process, but it is an important element in the chain of events that will lead you to your new position. While you are probably a talented, bright, and charming person, your resume may not reflect these qualities. A poorly written resume can get you nowhere; a well-written resume can land you an interview and potentially a job. A good resume can even lead the interviewer to ask you questions that will allow you to talk about your strengths and highlight the skills you can bring to a prospective employer. Even a person with very little experience can find a good job if he or she is assisted by a thoughtful and polished resume.

Lengthy, typewritten resumes are a thing of the past. Today, employers do not have the time or the patience for verbose documents; they look for tightly composed, straightforward, action-based resumes. Although a one-page resume is the norm, a two-page resume may be warranted if you have had extensive job experience or have changed careers and truly need the space to properly position yourself. If, after careful editing, you still need more than one page to present yourself, it's acceptable to use a second page. A crowded resume that's hard to read would be the worst of your choices.

Distilling your work experience, education, and interests into such a small space requires preparation and thought. This book takes you step-by-step through the process of crafting an effective resume that will stand out in today's competitive marketplace. It serves as a workbook and a place to write down your experiences, while also including the techniques you'll need to pull all the necessary elements together. In the following pages, you'll find many examples of resumes that are specific to your area of interest. Study them for inspiration and find what appeals to you. There are a variety of ways to organize and present your information; inside, you'll find several that will be suitable to your needs. Good luck landing the job of your dreams!

The Elements of an Effective Resume

An effective resume is composed of information that employers are most interested in knowing about a prospective job applicant. This information is conveyed by a few essential elements. The following is a list of elements that are found in most resumes—some essential, some optional. Later in this chapter, we will further examine the role of each of these elements in the makeup of your resume.

- Heading

- Objective and/or Keyword Section

- Work Experience

- Education

- Honors

- Activities

- Certificates and Licenses

- Publications

- Professional Memberships

- Special Skills

- Personal Information

- References

The first step in preparing your resume is to gather information about yourself and your past accomplishments. Later you will refine this information, rewrite it using effective language, and organize it into an attractive layout. But first, let's take a look at each of these important elements individually so you can judge their appropriateness for your resume.

Heading

Although the heading may seem to be the simplest section of your resume, be careful not to take it lightly. It is the first section your prospective employer will see, and it contains the information she or he will need to contact you. At the very least, the heading must contain your name, your home address, and, of course, a phone number where you can be reached easily.

In today's high-tech world, many of us have multiple ways that we can be contacted. You may list your e-mail address if you are reasonably sure the employer makes use of this form of communication. Keep in mind, however, that others may have access to your e-mail messages if you send them from an account provided by your current company. If this is a concern, do not list your work e-mail address on your resume. If you are able to take calls at your current place of business, you should include your work number, because most employers will attempt to contact you during typical business hours.

If you have voice mail or a reliable answering machine at home or at work, list its number in the heading and make sure your greeting is professional and clear. Always include at least one phone number in your heading, even if it is a temporary number, where a prospective employer can leave a message.

You might have a dozen different ways to be contacted, but you do not need to list all of them. Confine your numbers or addresses to those that are the easiest for the prospective employer to use and the simplest for you to retrieve.

Objective

When seeking a specific career path, it is important to list a job or career objective on your resume. This statement helps employers know the direction you see yourself taking, so they can determine whether your goals are in line with those of their organization and the position available. Normally, an objective is one to two sentences long. Its contents will vary depending on your career field, goals, and personality. The objective can be specific or general, but it should always be to the point. See the sample resumes in this book for examples.

If you are planning to use this resume online, or you suspect your potential employer is likely to scan your resume, you will want to include a "keyword" in the objective. This allows a prospective employer, searching hundreds of resumes for a specific skill or position objective, to locate the keyword and find your resume. In essence, a keyword is what's "hot" in your particular field at a given time. It's a buzzword, a shorthand way of getting a particular message across at a glance. For example, if you are a lawyer, your objective might state your desire to work in the area of corporate litigation. In this case, someone searching for the keyword "corporate litigation" will pull up your resume and know that you want to plan, research, and present cases at trial on behalf of the corporation. If your objective states that you "desire a challenging position in systems design," the keyword is "systems design," an industry-specific shorthand way of saying that you want to be involved in assessing the need for, acquiring, and implementing high-technology systems. These are keywords and every industry has them, so it's becoming more and more important to include a few in your resume. (You may need to conduct additional research to make sure you know what keywords are most likely to be used in your desired industry, profession, or situation.)

There are many resume and job-search sites online. Like most things in the online world, they vary a great deal in quality. Use your discretion. If you plan to apply for jobs online or advertise your availability this way, you will want to design a scannable resume. This type of resume uses a format that can be easily scanned into a computer and added to a database. Scanning allows a prospective employer to use keywords to quickly review each applicant's experience and skills, and (in the event that there are many candidates for the job) to keep your resume for future reference.

Many people find that it is worthwhile to create two or more versions of their basic resume. You may want an intricately designed resume on high-quality paper to mail or hand out *and* a resume that is designed to be scanned into a computer and saved on a database or an online job site. You can even create a resume in ASCII text to e-mail to prospective employers. For further information, you may wish to refer to the *Guide to Internet Job Searching*, by Frances Roehm and Margaret Dikel, updated and published every other year by McGraw-Hill. This excellent book contains helpful and detailed information about formatting a resume for Internet use. To get you started, in Chapter 3 we have included a list of things to keep in mind when creating electronic resumes.

Although it is usually a good idea to include an objective, in some cases this element is not necessary. The goal of the objective statement is to provide the employer with an idea of where you see yourself going in the field. However, if you are uncertain of the exact nature of the job you seek, including an objective that is too specific could result in your not being considered for a host of perfectly acceptable positions. If you decide not to use an objective heading in your resume, you should definitely incorporate the information that would be conveyed in the objective into your cover letter.

Work Experience

Work experience is arguably the most important element of them all. Unless you are a recent graduate or former homemaker with little or no relevant work experience, your current and former positions will provide the central focus of the resume. You will want this section to be as complete and carefully constructed as possible. By thoroughly examining your work experience, you can get to the heart of your accomplishments and present them in a way that demonstrates and highlights your qualifications.

If you are just entering the workforce, your resume will probably focus on your education, but you should also include information on your work or volunteer experiences. Although you will have less information about work experience than a person who has held multiple positions or is advanced in his or her career, the amount of information is not what is most important in this section. How the information is presented and what it says about you as a worker and a person are what really count.

As you create this section of your resume, remember the need for accuracy. Include all the necessary information about each of your jobs, including your job title, dates of employment, name of your employer, city, state, responsibilities, special projects you handled, and accomplishments. Be sure to list only accomplishments for which you were directly responsible. And don't be alarmed if you haven't participated in or worked on special projects, because this section may not be relevant to certain jobs.

The most common way to list your work experience is in *reverse chronological order*. In other words, start with your most recent job and work your way backward. This way, your prospective employer sees your current (and often most important) position before considering your past employment. Your most recent position, if it's the most important in terms of responsibilities and relevance to the job for which you are applying, should also be the one that includes the most information as compared to your previous positions.

Even if the work itself seems unrelated to your proposed career path, you should list any job or experience that will help sell your talents. If you were promoted or given greater responsibilities or commendations, be sure to mention the fact.

The following worksheet is provided to help you organize your experiences in the working world. It will also serve as an excellent resource to refer to when updating your resume in the future.

WORK EXPERIENCE

Job One:

Job Title _____

Dates _____

Employer _____

City, State _____

Major Duties _____

_____

_____

_____

_____

_____

_____

_____

Special Projects _____

_____

_____

_____

Accomplishments _____

_____

_____

_____

_____

Job Two:

Job Title _____

Dates _____

Employer _____

City, State _____

Major Duties _____

_____

_____

_____

_____

_____

_____

_____

Special Projects _____

_____

_____

_____

Accomplishments _____

_____

_____

_____

_____

_____

_____

_____

Job Three:

Job Title _____

Dates _____

Employer _____

City, State _____

Major Duties _____

_____

_____

_____

_____

_____

_____

_____

Special Projects _____

_____

_____

_____

Accomplishments _____

_____

_____

_____

_____

_____

_____

_____

_____

Job Four:

Job Title _____

Dates _____

Employer _____

City, State _____

Major Duties _____

_____

_____

_____

_____

_____

_____

_____

Special Projects _____

_____

_____

_____

Accomplishments _____

_____

_____

_____

_____

_____

_____

_____

Education

Education is usually the second most important element of a resume. Your educational background is often a deciding factor in an employer's decision to interview you. Highlight your accomplishments in school as much as you did those accomplishments at work. If you are looking for your first professional job, your education or life experience will be your greatest asset because your related work experience will be minimal. In this case, the education section becomes the most important means of selling yourself.

Include in this section all the degrees or certificates you have received; your major or area of concentration; all of the honors you earned; and any relevant activities you participated in, organized, or chaired. Again, list your most recent schooling first. If you have completed graduate-level work, begin with that and work your way back through your undergraduate education. If you have completed college, you generally should not list your high-school experience; do so only if you earned special honors, you had a grade point average that was much better than the norm, or this was your highest level of education.

If you have completed a large number of credit hours in a subject that may be relevant to the position you are seeking but did not obtain a degree, you may wish to list the hours or classes you completed. Keep in mind, however, that you may be asked to explain why you did not finish the program. If you are currently in school, list the degree, certificate, or license you expect to obtain and the projected date of completion.

The following worksheet will help you gather the information you need for this section of your resume.

EDUCATION

School One _____

Major or Area of Concentration _____

Degree _____

Dates _____

School Two _____

Major or Area of Concentration _____

Degree _____

Dates _____

Honors

If you include an honors section in your resume, you should highlight any awards, honors, or memberships in honorary societies that you have received. (You may also incorporate this information into your education section.) Often, the honors are academic in nature, but this section also may be used for special achievements in sports, clubs, or other school activities. Always include the name of the organization awarding the honor and the date(s) received. Use the following worksheet to help you gather your information.

HONORS

Honor One _____

Awarding Organization _____

Date(s) _____

Honor Two _____

Awarding Organization _____

Date(s) _____

Honor Three _____

Awarding Organization _____

Date(s) _____

Honor Four _____

Awarding Organization _____

Date(s) _____

Honor Five _____

Awarding Organization _____

Date(s) _____

Activities

Perhaps you have been active in different organizations or clubs; often an employer will look at such involvement as evidence of initiative, dedication, and good social skills. Examples of your ability to take a leading role in a group should be included on a resume, if you can provide them. The activities section of your resume should present neighborhood and community activities, volunteer positions, and so forth. In general, you may want to avoid listing any organization whose name indicates the race, creed, sex, age, marital status, sexual orientation, or nation of origin of its members because this could expose you to discrimination. Use the following worksheet to list the specifics of your activities.

ACTIVITIES

Organization/Activity _____

Accomplishments _____

_____

_____

Organization/Activity _____

Accomplishments _____

_____

_____

Organization/Activity _____

Accomplishments _____

_____

_____

As your work experience grows through the years, your school activities and honors will carry less weight and be emphasized less in your resume. Eventually, you will probably list only your degree and any major honors received. As time goes by, your job performance and the experience you've gained become the most important elements in your resume, which should change to reflect this.

Certificates and Licenses

If your chosen career path requires specialized training, you may already have certificates or licenses. You should list these if the job you are seeking requires them and you, of course, have acquired them. If you have applied for a license but have not yet received it, use the phrase "application pending."

License requirements vary by state. If you have moved or are planning to relocate to another state, check with that state's board or licensing agency for all licensing requirements.

Always make sure that all of the information you list is completely accurate. Locate copies of your certificates and licenses, and check the exact date and name of the accrediting agency. Use the following worksheet to organize the necessary information.

CERTIFICATES AND LICENSES

Name of License _____

Licensing Agency _____

Date Issued _____

Name of License _____

Licensing Agency _____

Date Issued _____

Name of License _____

Licensing Agency _____

Date Issued _____

Publications

Some professions strongly encourage or even require that you publish. If you have written, coauthored, or edited any books, articles, professional papers, or works of a similar nature that pertain to your field, you will definitely want to include this element. Remember to list the date of publication and the publisher's name, and specify whether you were the sole author or a coauthor. Book, magazine, or journal titles are generally italicized, while the titles of articles within a larger publication appear in quotes. (Check with your reference librarian for more about the appropriate way to present this information.) For scientific or research papers, you will need to give the date, place, and audience to whom the paper was presented.

Use the following worksheet to help you gather the necessary information about your publications.

PUBLICATIONS

Title and Type (Note, Article, etc.) _____

Title of Publication (Journal, Book, etc.) _____

Publisher _____

Date Published _____

Title and Type (Note, Article, etc.) _____

Title of Publication (Journal, Book, etc.) _____

Publisher _____

Date Published _____

Title and Type (Note, Article, etc.) _____

Title of Publication (Journal, Book, etc.) _____

Publisher _____

Date Published _____

Professional Memberships

Another potential element in your resume is a section listing professional memberships. Use this section to describe your involvement in professional associations, unions, and similar organizations. It is to your advantage to list any professional memberships that pertain to the job you are seeking. Many employers see your membership as representative of your desire to stay up-to-date and connected in your field. Include the dates of your involvement and whether you took part in any special activities or held any offices within the organization. Use the following worksheet to organize your information.

PROFESSIONAL MEMBERSHIPS

Name of Organization _____

Office(s) Held_____

Activities _____

Dates _____

Name of Organization _____

Office(s) Held_____

Activities _____

Dates _____

Name of Organization _____

Office(s) Held_____

Activities _____

Dates _____

Name of Organization _____

Office(s) Held_____

Activities _____

Dates _____

Special Skills

The special skills section of your resume is the place to mention any special abilities you have that relate to the job you are seeking. You can use this element to present certain talents or experiences that are not necessarily a part of your education or work experience. Common examples include fluency in a foreign language, extensive travel abroad, or knowledge of a particular computer application. "Special skills" can encompass a wide range of talents, and this section can be used creatively. However, for each skill you list, you should be able to describe how it would be a direct asset in the type of work you're seeking because employers may ask just that in an interview. If you can't think of a way to do this, it may be extraneous information.

Personal Information

Some people include personal information on their resumes. This is generally not recommended, but you might wish to include it if you think that something in your personal life, such as a hobby or talent, has some bearing on the position you are seeking. This type of information is often referred to at the beginning of an interview, when it may be used as an icebreaker. Of course, personal information regarding your age, marital status, race, religion, or sexual orientation should never appear on your resume as personal information. It should be given only in the context of memberships and activities, and only when doing so would not expose you to discrimination.

References

References are not usually given on the resume itself, but a prospective employer needs to know that you have references who may be contacted if necessary. All you need to include is a single sentence at the end of the resume: "References are available upon request," or even simply, "References available." Have a reference list ready—your interviewer may ask to see it! Contact each person on the list ahead of time to see whether it is all right for you to use him or her as a reference. This way, the person has a chance to think about what to say *before* the call occurs. This helps ensure that you will obtain the best reference possible.

Writing Your Resume

Now that you have gathered the information for each section of your resume, it's time to write it out in a way that will get the attention of the reviewer—hopefully, your future employer! The language you use in your resume will affect its success, so you must be careful and conscientious. Translate the facts you have gathered into the active, precise language of resume writing. You will be aiming for a resume that keeps the reader's interest and highlights your accomplishments in a concise and effective way.

Resume writing is unlike any other form of writing. Although your seventh-grade composition teacher would not approve, the rules of punctuation and sentence building are often completely ignored. Instead, you should try for a functional, direct writing style that focuses on the use of verbs and other words that imply action on your part. Writing with action words and strong verbs characterizes you to potential employers as an energetic, active person, someone who completes tasks and achieves results from his or her work. Resumes that do not make use of action words can sound passive and stale. These resumes are not effective and do not get the attention of any employer, no matter how qualified the applicant. Choose words that display your strengths and demonstrate your initiative. The following list of commonly used verbs will help you create a strong resume:

administered	assembled
advised	assumed responsibility
analyzed	billed
arranged	built

carried out	inspected
channeled	interviewed
collected	introduced
communicated	invented
compiled	maintained
completed	managed
conducted	met with
contacted	motivated
contracted	negotiated
coordinated	operated
counseled	orchestrated
created	ordered
cut	organized
designed	oversaw
determined	performed
developed	planned
directed	prepared
dispatched	presented
distributed	produced
documented	programmed
edited	published
established	purchased
expanded	recommended
functioned as	recorded
gathered	reduced
handled	referred
hired	represented
implemented	researched
improved	reviewed

saved	supervised
screened	taught
served as	tested
served on	trained
sold	typed
suggested	wrote

Let's look at two examples that differ only in their writing style. The first resume section is ineffective because it does not use action words to accent the applicant's work experiences.

WORK EXPERIENCE
Regional Sales Manager

Manager of sales representatives from seven states. Manager of twelve food chain accounts in the East. In charge of the sales force's planned selling toward specific goals. Supervisor and trainer of new sales representatives. Consulting for customers in the areas of inventory management and quality control.

Special Projects: Coordinator and sponsor of annual Food Industry Seminar.

Accomplishments: Monthly regional volume went up 25 percent during my tenure while, at the same time, a proper sales/cost ratio was maintained. Customer-company relations were improved.

In the following paragraph, we have rewritten the same section using action words. Notice how the tone has changed. It now sounds stronger and more active. This person accomplished goals and really *did* things.

WORK EXPERIENCE
Regional Sales Manager

Managed sales representatives from seven states. Oversaw twelve food chain accounts in the eastern United States. Directed the sales force in planned selling toward specific goals. Supervised and trained new sales representatives. Counseled customers in the areas of inventory management and quality control. Coordinated and sponsored the annual Food Industry Seminar. Increased monthly regional volume by 25 percent and helped to improve customer-company relations during my tenure.

One helpful way to construct the work experience section is to make use of your actual job descriptions—the written duties and expectations your employers have for a person in your current or former position. Job descriptions are rarely written in proper resume language, so you will have to rework them, but they do include much of the information necessary to create this section of your resume. If you have access to job descriptions for your former positions, you can use the details to construct an action-oriented paragraph. Often, your human resources department can provide a job description for your current position.

The following is an example of a typical human resources job description, followed by a rewritten version of the same description employing action words and specific details about the job. Again, pay attention to the style of writing instead of the content, as the details of your own experience will be unique.

WORK EXPERIENCE
Public Administrator I

Responsibilities: Coordinate and direct public services to meet the needs of the nation, state, or community. Analyze problems; work with special committees and public agencies; recommend solutions to governing bodies.

Aptitudes and Skills: Ability to relate to and communicate with people; solve complex problems through analysis; plan, organize, and implement policies and programs. Knowledge of political systems, financial management, personnel administration, program evaluation, and organizational theory.

WORK EXPERIENCE
Public Administrator I

Wrote pamphlets and conducted discussion groups to inform citizens of legislative processes and consumer issues. Organized and supervised 25 interviewers. Trained interviewers in effective communication skills.

After you have written out your resume, you are ready to begin the next important step: assembly and layout.

Chapter 3

Assembly and Layout

A t this point, you've gathered all the necessary information for your resume and rewritten it in language that will impress your potential employers. Your next step is to assemble the sections in a logical order and lay them out on the page neatly and attractively to achieve the desired effect: getting the interview.

Assembly

The order of the elements in a resume makes a difference in its overall effect. Clearly, you would not want to bury your name and address somewhere in the middle of the resume. Nor would you want to lead with a less important section, such as special skills. Put the elements in an order that stresses your most important accomplishments and the things that will be most appealing to your potential employer. For example, if you are new to the workforce, you will want the reviewer to read about your education and life skills before any part-time jobs you may have held for short durations. On the other hand, if you have been gainfully employed for several years and currently hold an important position in your company, you should list your work accomplishments ahead of your educational information, which has become less pertinent with time.

Certain things should always be included in your resume, but others are optional. The following list shows you which are which. You might want to use it as a checklist to be certain that you have included all of the necessary information.

Essential	**Optional**
Name	Cellular Phone Number
Address	Pager Number
Phone Number	E-Mail Address or Website Address
Work Experience	
Education	Voice Mail Number
References Phrase	Job Objective
	Honors
	Special Skills
	Publications
	Professional Memberships
	Activities
	Certificates and Licenses
	Personal Information
	Graphics
	Photograph

Your choice of optional sections depends on your own background and employment needs. Always use information that will put you in a favorable light—unless it's absolutely essential, avoid anything that will prompt the interviewer to ask questions about your weaknesses or something else that could be unflattering. Make sure your information is accurate and truthful. If your honors are impressive, include them in the resume. If your activities in school demonstrate talents that are necessary for the job you are seeking, allow space for a section on activities. If you are applying for a position that requires ornamental illustration, you may want to include border illustrations or graphics that demonstrate your talents in this area. If you are answering an advertisement for a job that requires certain physical traits, a photo of yourself might be appropriate. A person applying for a job as a computer programmer would *not* include a photo as part of his or her resume. Each resume is unique, just as each person is unique.

Types of Resumes

So far we have focused on the most common type of resume—the *reverse chronological* resume—in which your most recent job is listed first. This is the type of resume usually preferred by those who have to read a large number of resumes, and it is by far the most popular and widely circulated. However, this style of presentation may not be the most effective way to highlight *your* skills and accomplishments.

For example, if you are reentering the workforce after many years or are trying to change career fields, the *functional* resume may work best. This type of resume puts the focus on your achievements instead of the sequence of your work history. In the functional resume, your experience is presented through your general accomplishments and the skills you have developed in your working life.

A functional resume is assembled from the same information you gathered in Chapter 1. The main difference lies in how you organize the information. Essentially, the work experience section is divided in two, with your job duties and accomplishments constituting one section and your employers' names, cities, and states; your positions; and the dates employed making up the other. Place the first section near the top of your resume, just below your job objective (if used), and call it *Accomplishments* or *Achievements*. The second section, containing the bare essentials of your work history, should come after the accomplishments section and can be called *Employment History*, since it is a chronological overview of your former jobs.

The other sections of your resume remain the same. The work experience section is the only one affected in the functional format. By placing the section that focuses on your achievements at the beginning, you draw attention to these achievements. This puts less emphasis on where you worked and when, and more on what you did and what you are capable of doing.

If you are changing careers, the emphasis on skills and achievements is important. The identities of previous employers (who aren't part of your new career field) need to be downplayed. A functional resume can help accomplish this task. If you are reentering the workforce after a long absence, a functional resume is the obvious choice. And if you lack full-time work experience, you will need to draw attention away from this fact and put the focus on your skills and abilities. You may need to highlight your volunteer activities and part-time work. Education may also play a more important role in your resume.

The type of resume that is right for you will depend on your personal circumstances. It may be helpful to create both types and then compare them. Which one presents you in the best light? Examples of both types of resumes are included in this book. Use the sample resumes in Chapter 5 to help you decide on the content, presentation, and look of your own resume.

Resume or Curriculum Vitae?

A curriculum vitae (CV) is a longer, more detailed synopsis of your professional history, which generally runs three or more pages in length. It includes a summary of your educational and academic background as well as teaching and research experience, publications, presentations, awards, honors, affiliations, and other details. Because the purpose of the CV is different from that of the resume, many of the rules we've discussed thus far involving style and length do not apply.

A curriculum vitae is used primarily for admissions applications to graduate or professional schools, independent consulting in a variety of settings, proposals for fellowships or grants, or applications for positions in academia. As with a resume, you may need different versions of a CV for different types of positions. You should only send a CV when one is specifically requested by an employer or institution.

Like a resume, your CV should include your name, contact information, education, skills, and experience. In addition to the basics, a CV includes research and teaching experience, publications, grants and fellowships, professional associations and licenses, awards, and other information relevant to the position for which you are applying. You can follow the advice presented thus far to gather and organize your personal information.

Special Tips for Electronic Resumes

Because there are many details to consider in writing a resume that will be posted or transmitted on the Internet, or one that will be scanned into a computer when it is received, we suggest that you refer to the *Guide to Internet Job Searching*, by Frances Roehm and Margaret Dikel, as previously mentioned. However, here are some brief, general guidelines to follow if you expect your resume to be scanned into a computer.

- Use standard fonts in which none of the letters touch.

- Keep in mind that underlining, italics, and fancy scripts may not scan well.

- Use boldface and capitalization to set off elements. Again, make sure letters don't touch. Leave at least a quarter inch between lines of type.

- Keep information and elements at the left margin. Centering, columns, and even indenting may change when the resume is optically scanned.

- Do not use any lines, boxes, or graphics.

- Place the most important information at the top of the first page. If you use two pages, put "Page 1 of 2" at the bottom of the first page and put your name and "Page 2 of 2" at the top of the second page.

- List each telephone number on its own line in the header.

- Use multiple keywords or synonyms for what you do to make sure your qualifications will be picked up if a prospective employer is searching for them. Use nouns that are keywords for your profession.

- Be descriptive in your titles. For example, don't just use "assistant"; use "legal office assistant."

- Make sure the contrast between print and paper is good. Use a high-quality laser printer and white or very light colored 8½-by-11-inch paper.

- Mail a high-quality laser print or an excellent copy. Do not fold or use staples, as this might interfere with scanning. You may, however, use paper clips.

In addition to creating a resume that works well for scanning, you may want to have a resume that can be e-mailed to reviewers. Because you may not know what word processing application the recipient uses, the best format to use is ASCII text. (ASCII stands for "American Standard Code for Information Interchange.") It allows people with very different software platforms to exchange and understand information. (E-mail operates on this principle.) ASCII is a simple, text-only language, which means you can include only simple text. There can be no use of boldface, italics, or even paragraph indentations.

To create an ASCII resume, just use your normal word processing program; when finished, save it as a "text only" document. You will find this option under the "save" or "save as" command. Here is a list of things to *avoid* when crafting your electronic resume:

- Tabs. Use your space bar. Tabs will not work.

- Any special characters, such as mathematical symbols.

- Word wrap. Use hard returns (the return key) to make line breaks.

- Centering or other formatting. Align everything at the left margin.

- Bold or italic fonts. Everything will be converted to plain text when you save the file as a "text only" document.

Check carefully for any mistakes before you save the document as a text file. Spellcheck and proofread it several times; then ask someone with a keen eye to go over it again for you. Remember: the key is to keep it simple. Any attempt to make this resume pretty or decorative may result in a resume that is confusing and hard to read. After you have saved the document, you can cut and paste it into an e-mail or onto a website.

Layout for a Paper Resume

A great deal of care—and much more formatting—is necessary to achieve an attractive layout for your paper resume. There is no single appropriate layout that applies to every resume, but there are a few basic rules to follow in putting your resume on paper:

- Leave a comfortable margin on the sides, top, and bottom of the page (usually one to one and a half inches).

- Use appropriate spacing between the sections (two to three line spaces are usually adequate).

- Be consistent in the *type* of headings you use for different sections of your resume. For example, if you capitalize the heading EMPLOYMENT HISTORY, don't use initial capitals and underlining for a section of equal importance, such as Education.

- Do not use more than one font in your resume. Stay consistent by choosing a font that is fairly standard and easy to read, and don't change it for different sections. Beware of the tendency to try to make your resume original by choosing fancy type styles; your resume may end up looking unprofessional instead of creative. Unless you are in a very creative and artistic field, you should almost always stick with tried-and-true type styles like Times New Roman and Palatino, which are often used in business writing. In the area of resume styles, conservative is usually the best way to go.

CHRONOLOGICAL RESUME

RASHEED B. SMITH II

11 Hillcrest Drive • Columbia, SC 29202
(803) 555-1859 • rasheedsmith@xxx.com

EXPERIENCE

1999 - 2005
Equal Opportunity Program Specialist, U.S. Navy (E-7)
Classification: Chief Petty Officer
Duties: Advised officers on equal opportunity matters, provided training in nondiscrimination practices, assisted in formulating and revising equal opportunity directives, performed related duties

1994 - 1999
Personnelman, U.S. Navy (E-6)
Classification: Advanced from Personnelman Third Class to Personnelman First Class
Duties: Provided a variety of personnel-administration duties

1993 - 1994
Seaman, U.S. Navy (E-3)
Duties: Performed basic seamanship functions

EDUCATION

B.S., University of South Carolina, 2002
Major: Political Science
Minor: Sociology

Graduate, Defense Equal Opportunity Training Institute, 1997

Completed Navy Instructor Training Program, 1997

SKILLS

- Familiar with human resource best practices and management styles
- Trained on Microsoft Office and Lotus business software
- Completed several management-training courses on topics such as Goal Setting, Conflict Resolution, and Mentoring

REFERENCES

Available on request

FUNCTIONAL RESUME

WILLIAM K. BROWN

615 Cardinal Drive
Fergus Falls, MN 56537
(218) 555-0464 (voice)
(218) 555-1855 (fax)
williambrown@xxx.com

CAREER OBJECTIVE

A position in surveying or topographic engineering.

RELATED SKILLS AND EXPERIENCE

- Highly skilled topographic surveyor with 15 years' experience in the United States Army.
- Achieved advanced skill level through extensive field experience and Army training courses.
- Thoroughly familiar with the most effective contemporary surveying methods, including use of various types of surveying equipment.

WORK BACKGROUND

As Army topographic surveyor, performed tasks such as the following:
- Recorded topographic survey data.
- Operated a variety of survey instruments.
- Performed topographic and geodetic computations.
- Interpreted maps and aerial photographs.
- Performed a wide range of computations including horizontal differences, angular closures, and triangulations.
- Supervised other workers including topographic-instrument-repair specialists.
- Supervised programming of electronic calculators.
- Prepared technical and personnel reports.

TRAINING/EDUCATION

Completed military training in mathematics, surveying, engineering computations, technical writing, optics, data processing, and related areas.

References Available on Request

- Always try to fit your resume on one page. If you are having trouble with this, you may be trying to say too much. Edit out any repetitive or unnecessary information, and shorten descriptions of earlier jobs where possible. Ask a friend you trust for feedback on what seems unnecessary or unimportant. For example, you may have included too many optional sections. Today, with the prevalence of the personal computer as a tool, there is no excuse for a poorly laid out resume. Experiment with variations until you are pleased with the result.

Remember that a resume is not an autobiography. Too much information will only get in the way. The more compact your resume, the easier it will be to review. If a person who is swamped with resumes looks at yours, catches the main points, and then calls you for an interview to fill in some of the details, your resume has already accomplished its task. A clear and concise resume makes for a happy reader and a good impression.

There are times when, despite extensive editing, the resume simply cannot fit on one page. In this case, the resume should be laid out on two pages in such a way that neither clarity nor appearance is compromised. Each page of a two-page resume should be marked clearly: the first should indicate "Page 1 of 2," and the second should include your name and the page number, for example, "Julia Ramirez—Page 2 of 2." The pages should then be paper-clipped together. You may use a smaller type size (in the same font as the body of your resume) for the page numbers. Place them at the bottom of page one and the top of page two. Again, spend the time now to experiment with the layout until you find one that looks good to you.

Always show your final layout to other people and ask them what they like or dislike about it, and what impresses them most when they read your resume. Make sure that their responses are the same as what you want to elicit from your prospective employer. If they aren't the same, you should continue to make changes until the necessary information is emphasized.

Proofreading

After you have finished typing the master copy of your resume and before you have it copied or printed, thoroughly check it for typing and spelling errors. Do not place all your trust in your computer's spellcheck function. Use an old editing trick and read the whole resume backward—start at the end and read it right to left and bottom to top. This can help you see the small errors or inconsistencies that are easy to overlook. Take time to do it right because a single error on a document this important can cause the reader to judge your attention to detail in a harsh light.

Have several people look at the finished resume just in case you've missed an error. Don't try to take a shortcut; not having an unbiased set of eyes examine your resume now could mean embarrassment later. Even experienced editors can easily overlook their own errors. Be thorough and conscientious with your proofreading so your first impression is a perfect one.

We have included the following rules of capitalization and punctuation to assist you in the final stage of creating your resume. Remember that resumes often require use of a shorthand style of writing that may include sentences without periods and other stylistic choices that break the standard rules of grammar. Be consistent in each section and throughout the whole resume with your choices.

RULES OF CAPITALIZATION

- Capitalize proper nouns, such as names of schools, colleges, and universities; names of companies; and brand names of products.

- Capitalize major words in the names and titles of books, tests, and articles that appear in the body of your resume.

- Capitalize words in major section headings of your resume.

- Do not capitalize words just because they seem important.

- When in doubt, consult a style manual such as *Words into Type* (Prentice Hall) or *The Chicago Manual of Style* (The University of Chicago Press). Your local library can help you locate these and other reference books. Many computer programs also have grammar help sections.

RULES OF PUNCTUATION

- Use commas to separate words in a series.

- Use a semicolon to separate series of words that already include commas within the series. (For an example, see the first rule of capitalization.)

- Use a semicolon to separate independent clauses that are not joined by a conjunction.

- Use a period to end a sentence.

- Use a colon to show that examples or details follow that will expand or amplify the preceding phrase.

- Avoid the use of dashes.

- Avoid the use of brackets.

- If you use any punctuation in an unusual way in your resume, be consistent in its use.

- Whenever you are uncertain, consult a style manual.

Putting Your Resume in Print

You will need to buy high-quality paper for your printer before you print your finished resume. Regular office paper is not good enough for resumes; the reviewer will probably think it looks flimsy and cheap. Go to an office supply store or copy shop and select a high-quality bond paper that will make a good first impression. Select colors like white, off-white, or possibly a light gray. In some industries, a pastel may be acceptable, but be sure the color and feel of the paper make a subtle, positive statement about you. Nothing in the choice of paper should be loud or unprofessional.

If your computer printer does not reproduce your resume properly and produces smudged or stuttered type, either ask to borrow a friend's or take your disk (or a clean original) to a printer or copy shop for high-quality copying. If you anticipate needing a large number of copies, taking your resume to a copy shop or a printer is probably the best choice.

Hold a sheet of your unprinted bond paper up to the light. If it has a watermark, you will want to point this out to the person helping you with copies; the printing should be done so that the reader can read the print and see the watermark the right way up. Check each copy for smudges or streaks. This is the time to be a perfectionist—the results of your careful preparation will be well worth it.

The Cover Letter

Once your resume has been assembled, laid out, and printed to your satisfaction, the next and final step before distribution is to write your cover letter. Though there may be instances where you deliver your resume in person, you will usually send it through the mail or online. Resumes sent through the mail always need an accompanying letter that briefly introduces you and your resume. The purpose of the cover letter is to get a potential employer to read your resume, just as the purpose of the resume is to get that same potential employer to call you for an interview.

Like your resume, your cover letter should be clean, neat, and direct. A cover letter usually includes the following information:

1. Your name and address (unless it already appears on your personal letterhead) and your phone number(s); see item 7.

2. The date.

3. The name and address of the person and company to whom you are sending your resume.

4. The salutation ("Dear Mr." or "Dear Ms." followed by the person's last name, or "To Whom It May Concern" if you are answering a blind ad).

5. An opening paragraph explaining why you are writing (for example, in response to an ad, as a follow-up to a previous meeting, at the suggestion of someone you both know) and indicating that you are interested in whatever job is being offered.

6. One or more paragraphs that tell why you want to work for the company and what qualifications and experiences you can bring to the position. This is a good place to mention some detail about

that particular company that makes you want to work for them; this shows that you have done some research before applying.

7. A final paragraph that closes the letter and invites the reviewer to contact you for an interview. This can be a good place to tell the potential employer which method would be best to use when contacting you. Be sure to give the correct phone number and a good time to reach you, if that is important. You may mention here that your references are available upon request.

8. The closing ("Sincerely" or "Yours truly") followed by your signature in a dark ink, with your name typed under it.

Your cover letter should include all of this information and be no longer than one page in length. The language used should be polite, businesslike, and to the point. Don't attempt to tell your life story in the cover letter; a long and cluttered letter will serve only to annoy the reader. Remember that you need to mention only a few of your accomplishments and skills in the cover letter. The rest of your information is available in your resume. If your cover letter is a success, your resume will be read and all pertinent information reviewed by your prospective employer.

Producing the Cover Letter

Cover letters should always be individualized because they are always written to specific individuals and companies. Never use a form letter for your cover letter or copy it as you would a resume. Each cover letter should be unique, and as personal and lively as possible. (Of course, once you have written and rewritten your first cover letter until you are satisfied with it, you can certainly use similar wording in subsequent letters. You may want to save a template on your computer for future reference.) Keep a hard copy of each cover letter so you know exactly what you wrote in each one.

There are sample cover letters in Chapter 6. Use them as models or for ideas of how to assemble and lay out your own cover letters. Remember that every letter is unique and depends on the particular circumstances of the individual writing it and the job for which he or she is applying.

After you have written your cover letter, proofread it as thoroughly as you did your resume. Again, spelling or punctuation errors are a sure sign of carelessness, and you don't want that to be a part of your first impression on a prospective employer. This is no time to trust your spellcheck function. Even after going through a spelling and grammar check, your cover letter should be carefully proofread by at least one other person.

Print the cover letter on the same quality bond paper you used for your resume. Remember to sign it, using a good dark-ink pen. Handle the letter and resume carefully to avoid smudging or wrinkling, and mail them together in an appropriately sized envelope. Many stores sell matching envelopes to coordinate with your choice of bond paper.

Keep an accurate record of all resumes you send out and the results of each mailing. This record can be kept on your computer, in a calendar or notebook, or on file cards. Knowing when a resume is likely to have been received will keep you on track as you make follow-up phone calls.

About a week after mailing resumes and cover letters to potential employers, contact them by telephone. Confirm that your resume arrived and ask whether an interview might be possible. Be sure to record the name of the person you spoke to and any other information you gleaned from the conversation. It is wise to treat the person answering the phone with a great deal of respect; sometimes the assistant or receptionist has the ear of the person doing the hiring.

You should make a great impression with the strong, straightforward resume and personalized cover letter you have just created. We wish you every success in securing the career of your dreams!

Sample Resumes

This chapter contains dozens of sample resumes for people pursuing a wide variety of jobs following their military service.

There are many different styles of resumes in terms of graphic layout and presentation of information. These samples represent people with varying amounts of education and experience. Use them as models for your own resume. Choose one resume or borrow elements from several different resumes to help you construct your own.

Daryl S. Kaufman

303 Fairfax Avenue
Charleston, WV 25302
(304) 555-4685 (voice)
(304) 555-4695 (fax)
darylkaufman@xxx.com

PROFESSIONAL OBJECTIVE
Challenging position as a caseworker or counselor

EDUCATION
Associate in Applied Science
Marshall University, 2004
Huntington, WV
Major: Social Work
Completed additional training at Naval Drug Rehabilitation Center, San Diego, CA

EXPERIENCE
- U.S. Navy 1998 - 2004
  Served in a counseling capacity, specializing in drug and alcohol counseling
- Marshall University, Huntington, WV, 2002 - present
  Part-time counseling assistant, assigned to student health center

SPECIAL SKILLS/COMPETENCIES
- Adept at working with people
- Experienced in counseling persons with various problems/needs
- Skilled in interviewing techniques, administration and scoring of psychological tests, and other counseling strategies
- Experienced in screening and evaluating persons with substance abuse problems and assisting in managing substance abuse programs
- Certification: LCSW, CSWM, both in West Virginia

References are available on request.

JAMES P. WODYNSKI

212 Harding Avenue • Evanston, IL 60201 • (847) 555-2530
jameswodynski@xxx.com

EXPERIENCE

Enlisted Personnel, United States Coast Guard
Ratings Held: Progressed from Seaman Recruit (E-l) to Radarman First Class (E-6)
Active Service: 1999–2005
Reserve Duty: Present
Duties: Operated radar and associated equipment
Representative Tasks Completed:
- Collected, processed, displayed, evaluated, and disseminated information related to movement of ships, aircraft, and other objects
- Performed duties related to navigation and piloting
- Prepared and maintained records and logs for Combat Information Center operations and operating equipment
- Understood and used *Nautical Rules of the Road*
- Prepared requisitions for supplies
- Computed statistics necessary for operational reports
- Prepared preventive-maintenance schedules

EDUCATIONAL BACKGROUND

Graduate, Yorktown Training Center, VA
Successfully completed additional Coast Guard courses including Radioman First Class (Course No. 139-5) via Coast Guard Institute, Oklahoma City, OK

SPECIAL SKILLS

Excellent quantitative skills
Adept at use of various computer software, including MS Office, Lotus Notes, and AutoCAD

REFERENCES PROVIDED ON REQUEST

CARLETTA A. WILLIAMS
2821 Crown Drive
Conway, South Carolina 29526
(803) 555-2833
carlettawilliams@xxx.com

SUMMARY OF EXPERIENCE
- Served 12 years in the United States Army
- Progressed to rank of Warrant Officer
- Specialized in maintaining and operating field artillery radars to provide target location

TECHNICAL AREAS OF EXPERTISE
- Knowledge of effective practices in management and supervision
- Knowledge of operational aspects of field artillery
- Close familiarity with technical principles of equipment construction
- Understanding of safety applications relevant to operations and maintenance
- Solid understanding of basic electronics theory

EMPLOYMENT HISTORY
U.S. Army, 1998–2004
Position: Target Acquisition Radar Technician
Served with distinction including postings at the following:
    Fort Knox, Kentucky
    Fort Sill, Oklahoma
    Operation Desert Storm (Persian Gulf)
    Fort Jackson, South Carolina
Rank: Warrant Officer
Awards: Received several medals and commendations; listing and complete military record available on request

EDUCATION
Associate Degree, Jefferson Community College, Louisville, Kentucky, 1998 (general studies)
Graduate, Army Field Artillery School, 1999

MEMBERSHIPS
Member, Women's Leadership Association

REFERENCES
Available on request

Robert Wilcox
1805 Grayland Avenue
Price, UT 84501
(801) 555-1918 home phone   (801) 555-9089 cell phone
robertwilcox@xxx.com

Employment Objective

Position in the telephone, power, or cable industry

Related Experience

Line Installer and Repairer, U.S. Navy, 1999–2005
Performed a variety of duties involved in installing, maintaining, and
repairing electrical cables and communication lines, including:
- Erecting utility poles
- Operating mechanical lift, plow, and other equipment
- Installing overhead communications and electrical cable between
  utility poles
- Installing street lights and other lighting systems
- Splicing and sealing cables for watertightness
- Installing voltage regulators and electrical transformers
- Related duties

Computer Experience

Microsoft Office (Word, Outlook, Excel)
Basic Web-searching skills

Additionally, very comfortable learning new technologies

Education

Completed special training including program in cable splicing and
repair at Navy Construction Training Center, Port Hueneme, CA, 1999

References available on request

◆ LYNN VALENTINE

1218 Grove Avenue
Marquette, MI 49855
(906) 555-8228
lynnvalentine@xxx.com

Career Objective:

Position in Optical Technology or related area.

Professional Accomplishments:

Served in the United States Army as an Optical Laboratory Specialist. In this capacity, performed duties including the following:

- ◆ Made and duplicated prescription lenses
- ◆ Performed various tasks such as selecting proper stock to fulfill requirements, computing and recording curvature and thickness, edging lenses to correct size and shape, selecting and assembling lens frame components, mounting lenses and aligning frames, completing various calculations
- ◆ Maintained records of prescriptions and inventory of supplies and equipment using Excel spreadsheets
- ◆ Supervised junior personnel
- ◆ Assigned duties and trained subordinates
- ◆ Supervised quality-control procedures
- ◆ Completed administrative reports
- ◆ Earned outstanding performance ratings

Military Service Record:

Active Duty, 1998–2005
U.S. Army Reserve, Present
Received several awards and commendations. Complete service record available at your request.

Educational Background:

Associate Degree, Midlands Technical College, Columbia, SC, 2003
Grade point average: 3.5 (4-point scale)
Additional specialized training in Army courses included optical laboratory procedures, information management, personnel supervision, and organizational management.

References Available

HARRISON TILLMAN

420 Reagan Road
Fort Smith, AR 72913
(501) 555-0409
harrisontillman@xxx.com

EXPERIENCE

Pharmacy Specialist, United States Army, 1998 - 2004.
Clerk, Goodson's Drugs, Little Rock, AR, 1994 - 1998 (part-time).

EDUCATION

Pursuing a B.S. at the University of Arkansas (degree anticipated 2006).

Graduate, Medical Field Service School, Fort Sam Houston, TX, 2003. Successfully completed 715-hour training program in providing auxiliary pharmacy services.

Diploma, George Washington High School, Little Rock, AR, 2001. Honor roll student.

PROFESSIONAL SKILLS

- Provided support to pharmacists and physicians by preparing, controlling, and issuing pharmaceutical products.
- Assisted pharmacists in performing a wide range of duties.
- Compounded and filled prescription orders.
- Performed storage, accounting, inventory, and control procedures.
- Issued medications under pharmacists' supervision.
- Assisted in pharmacy inspections.
- Maintained stock levels and ordered supplies.
- Performed other related duties.

RECOGNITIONS

Earned several awards including Army Good Conduct Medal and Superior Unit Award.
Received excellent evaluations from superiors.

REFERENCES

Available on request.

DONALD P. SPOONER

88 Meadowview Townhomes
Fort Lauderdale, Florida 33301
(305) 555-1692 home
(305) 555-5467 cellular
donaldspooner@xxx.com

CAREER OBJECTIVE

To obtain a position in the construction industry utilizing skills and experience gained as an experienced carpenter

EDUCATION

- Graduate, U.S. Army Engineer School, Fort Leonard Wood, Missouri (eight-week training course in carpentry/masonry)
- High school diploma with vocational training in construction, Wilson High School, Fort Lauderdale, Florida

RELATED EXPERIENCE

- Fabricated, erected, and maintained/repaired wooden and masonry structures on U.S. Army bases
- Attained advanced skill level and provided technical guidance and supervision of other personnel
- Performed complex construction activities including interpreting blueprints, estimating material needs, and installing finished carpentry product
- Mastered use of a variety of tools including power tools
- Performed a comprehensive array of tasks including erection of building components such as floors, roofing systems, walls, and stairs
- Completed both rough and finish work while working in a timely fashion

REFERENCES PROVIDED ON REQUEST

Harshad Singh

1056 King Street Extension
Huntington, IN 46750
(219) 555-8465 home phone
(219) 555-3657 cellular phone
harshadsingh@xxx.com

PROFESSIONAL EXPERIENCE

Seven years' experience in the United States Army (1998 - 2005), specializing as a parachute rigger

Tours of duty in both Afghanistan and Iraq

JOB DUTIES
- Packed both aircraft cargo and personnel parachutes
- Fabricated, assembled, and rigged airdrop equipment
- Loaded, positioned, and secured cargo for airdrop to troops in Iraq and Afghanistan
- Inspected and inventoried airdrop equipment
- Provided technical guidance to less-experienced personnel
- Tested rip cord and canopy-release assemblies
- Conducted inspections of airdrop equipment

SKILLS
- Conscientious worker
- Attentive to detail
- Able to comprehend and teach complex instructions
- Flexible and easily adaptable to changing conditions

EDUCATION

Graduate, Quartermaster School, Ft. Lee, VA, 2002
   396-hour course in advanced parachute rigging

Graduate, Jefferson High School, Huntington, IN, 1998

REFERENCES
Available on request

DAVID C. SCHULZ
1308 Ellis Road
Glendale, AZ 85306
(602) 555-5121 home phone
(602) 555-5673 cellular phone
davidschulz@xxx.com

OBJECTIVE

A position in financial management, warehousing, logistics management, purchasing, or a related field.

RELEVANT SKILLS AND EXPERIENCE

Fifteen years' experience in the United States Coast Guard, specializing in finance and supply (1990 - 2005). At time of retirement, had progressed to rank of Warrant Officer.
➤ Served as a technical specialist in finance and supply
➤ Planned, organized, and supervised the work of storekeepers, subsistence specialists, and other finance and supply personnel
➤ Supervised the inventory of supplies and equipment
➤ Planned and supervised the preparation of budgets, payrolls, and other information
➤ Coordinated preparation for regular audits
➤ Directed the organization and upkeep of department records

SPECIAL TRAINING

Military courses, seminars, and college courses completed in these areas:
➤ Accounting Systems
➤ Principles of Management
➤ Technical Communications
➤ Logistics Management
➤ Personnel Supervision
➤ Fundamentals of Purchasing and Supply
➤ Budget Processes
➤ Excel Spreadsheets

REFERENCES ON REQUEST

JUAN SANCHEZ

3838 16th Street

San Bernardino, CA 92401

(714) 555-6155

juansanchez@xxx.com

OBJECTIVE
Responsible position requiring proven mechanical skills

ACHIEVEMENTS
- Provided comprehensive mechanical services for military aircraft.
- Received excellent evaluations from superiors.
- Earned three promotions in rank based on job accomplishments and overall performance.

WORK EXPERIENCE
United States Coast Guard, 1999–2005
Specialty: Aircraft maintenance and repair
Rating: Aviation Structural Mechanic First Class (E-6)
Responsibilities:
- Performed comprehensive duties related to handling, inspecting, servicing, and maintaining aircraft structures and components.
- Fabricated and assembled metal parts.
- Made repairs.
- Performed nondestructive testing.
- Painted and maintained painting equipment.
- Maintained hydraulic systems, landing gear, fuel tanks, and other components.
- Performed related duties.

EDUCATION
Graduate, Aviation Training Technical Center, USCG, Elizabeth City, NC, 2001
Diploma, Warren High School, San Bernardino, CA, 1999

REFERENCES
Available on request

TYRONE H. ROBERTS
17 N. Franklin St.
Valencia, CA 91355
(805) 555-5145
tyroneroberts@xxx.com

EMPLOYMENT OBJECTIVE

To obtain a position involving installation or repair of electrical systems and components

CAREER HISTORY

• Ten years' outstanding service maintaining and repairing aircraft electrical systems in the United States Marine Corps
• Honorably discharged at rank of Sergeant (E-5) after service as Aircraft Electrical Systems Technician, 2005

WORK BACKGROUND

• Installed and repaired electrical components and systems on military aircraft
• Inspected and tested electrical components
• Diagnosed equipment malfunctions
• Demonstrated thorough working knowledge of diodes, transistors, integrated circuits, motors, and other electrical components
• Performed Level 3 tasks including conducting preflight and postflight operational tests on electrical systems

SKILLS

• Comfortable reading electronic schematics
• Able to learn new technology
• Detail-oriented

REFERENCES PROVIDED ON REQUEST

❖ Dennis R. Riley ❖

606 Tall Oaks Lane ❖ Helena, MT 59624
(406) 555-6540 ❖ dennisriley@xxx.com

Career Objective
Position as a civilian pilot or in a management/support role within the aviation industry

Education
- ❖ M.S. in Management, Georgetown University, Washington, DC, 2004
- ❖ B.S., United States Air Force Academy, 2000
  Graduated in top 20 percent of class

Military Experience
- ❖ Highly experienced as accomplished pilot on active duty with the U.S. Air Force (1990–2003)
- ❖ Experienced in flying a variety of aircraft, with emphasis on the F-16 and comprehensive training as a combat pilot
- ❖ Active participant in Operation Iraqi Freedom with several medals/citations (complete list available)
- ❖ Highly skilled in all aspects of aircraft operation
- ❖ Exemplary military record with option to continue in service still available at time of leaving military

Special Knowledge and Skills
- ❖ Highly analytical
- ❖ Flexible in taking on new assignments
- ❖ Diligent in applying sound safety skills to all aspects of aviation practice and management

Memberships
- ❖ Aviation Society of America
- ❖ Rotary International

References available on request

COLLEEN QUINN

3104 Linden Court • Bradford, MA 01830
Home: (508) 555-9576 • Cellular: (508) 555-0909
E-mail: cquinn@xxx.com

CAREER OBJECTIVE

A position in computer repair, installation, or service

PROFESSIONAL EXPERIENCE

- Served in U.S. Army, 1995–2005; specialized in servicing and repairing computer systems supporting advanced communications equipment
- Installed computers and computer systems as well as a wide variety of software
- Diagnosed equipment problems and identified equipment malfunctions
- Installed printers and other peripheral devices
- Serviced and replaced components of computers and related equipment
- Transported computer equipment to and from repair locations, as well as performing work on-site
- Maintained up-to-date knowledge of advancements in computer technology

MILITARY SERVICE BACKGROUND

- Reached rank of Sergeant
- Earned excellent performance evaluations

EDUCATION

- Successfully completed 1,036-hour training course in Automated Computer Systems Repair at Fort Gordon, GA
- Completed 30 semester hours in computer technology, electronics, and related subjects at Aiken Technical College, Aiken, SC, and Jefferson Community College, Lexington, KY
- Completed additional correspondence courses and other Army training courses
- Certified Microsoft Specialist
- Oracle Certification

References, including complete military records, are available upon request.

RASHEED B. SMITH II

11 Hillcrest Drive • Columbia, SC 29202 • (803) 555-1859
rasheedsmith@xxx.com

EXPERIENCE	1999 - 2005 Equal Opportunity Program Specialist, U.S. Navy (E-7) Classification: Chief Petty Officer Duties: Advised officers on equal opportunity matters, provided training in nondiscrimination practices, assisted in formulating and revising equal opportunity directives, performed related duties
	1994 - 1999 Personnelman, U.S. Navy (E-6) Classification: Advanced from Personnelman Third Class to Personnelman First Class Duties: Provided a variety of personnel-administration duties
	1993 - 1994 Seaman, U.S. Navy (E-3) Duties: Performed basic seamanship functions
EDUCATION	B.S., University of South Carolina, 2002 Major: Political Science Minor: Sociology Graduate, Defense Equal Opportunity Training Institute, 1997 Completed Navy Instructor Training Program, 1997
SKILLS	• Familiar with human resource best practices and management styles • Trained on Microsoft Office and Lotus business software • Completed several management-training courses on topics such as goal setting, conflict resolution, and mentoring
REFERENCES	Available on request

JASON RASKIN

1005 University Blvd.
Fort Collins, CO 80523
(303) 555-6922
jasonraskin@xxx.com

CAREER OBJECTIVE
To obtain a position in auto body repair

RELATED EXPERIENCE
Experienced in repairing frames and bodies of trucks, automobiles, and other vehicles; also, skilled in using a wide range of tools and equipment

Experienced in tasks such as:
- Replacing damaged body parts
- Straightening frames, doors, hoods, and fenders
- Welding damaged frames and auto body parts
- Installing glass windows
- Refinishing body surfaces
- Completing other related tasks

WORK BACKGROUND
Served in United States Army, 1998–2005
- Specialized in providing auto body repair services for Army vehicles
- Worked well with diverse personnel

Webb Auto Repair, 1996–1998 (part-time and summers)
Fort Collins, CO
- Provided general services ranging from cleanup to assisting in basic auto body repair functions; range of duties progressed during job tenure

TRAINING
Completed certificate in auto body repair, Rocky Mountain Technical College, 1995

Completed additional training through military courses relating specifically to motor pool maintenance

REFERENCES PROVIDED ON REQUEST

ROBERTO A. REYES
1378 Orchard Street NE
Santa Fe, NM 87501
(505) 555-4056
robertoreyes@xxx.com

WORK EXPERIENCE	2002 - present Infantry Senior Sergeant, U.S. Army Serve as principal operations officer of an infantry brigade. 1999 - 2002 Infantryman, U.S. Army Performed basic functions necessary as a member of a highly trained combat brigade. 1998 - 1999 Store clerk, J-Mart Corporation, Santa Fe, NM Stocked merchandise and checked out customers.
EDUCATION	1999 - 2004 Completed several Army training courses. June 1998 Diploma, Anderson High School, Santa Fe, NM
SPECIAL SKILLS	• Experienced, proven leader. • Provided day-to-day leadership to enlisted personnel in carrying out complex, highly difficult assignments requiring both physical fitness and problem-solving capabilities, with combat experience in Afghanistan. • Earned commendations for leadership, marksmanship, and other job-performance factors. • Able to adapt to rapidly changing situations.
REFERENCES	Provided on request.

Ricardo Vasquez

15 Orchard Court Drive
Baltimore, Maryland 21202
Home: (301) 555-1218
Cellular: (301) 555-9087
E-mail: ricardo.vasquez@xxx.com

Summary of Qualifications

Experienced and highly competent dental hygienist. Adept at interacting with people and creating a nonthreatening environment.

Accomplishments

Served successfully on active duty with the United States Navy as a dental hygienist. Received outstanding performance evaluations. Helped unit earn citation for excellence, 2000 and 2001. Served in volunteer capacity through special program providing dental care for disadvantaged children, 2003 - 2005.

Employment History

1996 - 2005 Dental Hygienist, United States Navy
Rank: Petty Officer First Class

Locations of service:
U.S. Naval Station, Agana, Guam, 2003 - 2005
Naval Medical Command, Bethesda, Maryland, 1996 - 2003

Education

Associate in Science degree (Dental Hygiene), 1996
Towson State University
Baltimore, Maryland 21204
GPA: 3.75 (4.0 scale)
Member, student government

Certificates/Licenses

Certified, National Dental Hygiene Board
Certified, Mid-Atlantic Regional Dental Hygiene Board

Memberships

Member, American Dental Hygiene Association
Member, Maryland Dental Hygiene Society
Member, Local United Way Advisory Committee

References

Provided on request.

STUART PURDY JR.

Route 4, Box 189 • Winfield, KS 67156
(316) 555-0370 home • (316) 555-9676 cellular
stuartpurdy@xxx.com

EMPLOYMENT HISTORY:

2000–2005 Recruiter, U.S. Army
1996–2000 Infantryman, U.S. Army
1994–1996 Sales Associate, Wilson Insurance Company, Winfield, KS

EXPERIENCE SUMMARY:

- As Army recruiter, contacted and interviewed individuals as potential enlistees
- Contacted representatives of schools and coordinated recruiting visits
- Presented formal and informal talks to various groups
- Started a chat room for prospective recruits to ask questions and talk about the military
- Distributed publicity materials
- Conducted market research and analysis
- Maintained contact with prospective recruits through e-mail and telephone, storing information in an Excel spreadsheet that I developed
- Routinely surpassed recruiting goals through efficiency and follow-through
- Updated recruiting station's Web page with recruiting activities and other information
- Fluent in Spanish

EDUCATION:

Graduate, Recruiting and Retention School
Ft. Benjamin Harrison, IN, 2000

MEMBERSHIPS:

Toastmasters International
Computer Club, Army

REFERENCES:

Available on request

Louise Pruette

Route 2, Box 21A • Jackson Heights, MS 39212

(601) 555-1574 (voice) • (601) 555-1145 (fax)

louise-pruette@xxx.com

Position Desired
Position in business management

Work Experience
U.S. Army, 1999–2005
Rank: Captain
Specialty: Armament Material Management

Duties
- Managed logistical functions.
- Supervised warehouse and transportation personnel.
- Performed planning, quality assurance, evaluation, and related duties as part of Army support unit providing munitions and supplies.

Education
Master of Business Administration, Clemson University, Clemson, SC, 2004

Bachelor of Business Administration, Radford University, Radford, VA, 1999
   Also successfully completed Army R.O.T.C. program
   Member, Alpha Kappa Tau Business Honor Society

Memberships
Member, U.S. Army Reserve
Member, American Logistics Management Association

References
Provided on request

■ DONALD E. PFEIFER ■

3188 Bradshaw Road
Manchester, CT 06040
(203) 555-1286 home office
(203) 555-8787 cellular
donaldpfeifer@xxx.com

EMPLOYMENT OBJECTIVE

To obtain a position in graphic design or related area requiring advanced design and illustration skills

RELATED SKILLS AND EXPERIENCE

- Highly experienced in graphic design and illustration
- Experienced in various techniques for developing illustrations for posters, graphs, charts, training aids, brochures, books, and other publications using Photoshop, Illustrator, Freehand, and Acrobat
- Accomplished in using a variety of media including pencil, pen and ink, watercolor, and art markers
- Skilled in producing both realistic and cartoon-style drawings and other illustrations
- Experienced in using a wide range of equipment including copy cameras, orthographic equipment, and other graphics arts and audiovisual presentation equipment
- Highly flexible in completing different types of assignments, working with others, and using creativity in practical applications

WORK BACKGROUND

1997–2005
Chief Illustrator Draftsman (E-7), United States Navy.

- Honorably discharged after nine years of service; decided against reenlistment in favor of civilian life
- Received several promotions and recognitions; complete military record available on request
- Portfolio also available online: donaldpfeifer.xxx

REFERENCES PROVIDED ON REQUEST

PAULA L. PATTERSON, M.D.

2311 Lawrence Street
Emmitsburg, MD 21727
(301) 555-6122
paula-patterson@xxx.com

OBJECTIVE
A position in medical research

EDUCATION
M.D., University of Virginia School of Medicine, Charlottesville, VA, 1996

M.S., University of Virginia, Charlottesville, VA, 1992
Major: Biology
4.0 grade point average

B.S., Virginia Tech, Blacksburg, VA, 1991
Major: Chemistry
Minor: Biology
3.9 (4.0 scale) grade point average

PROFESSIONAL EXPERIENCE
Active Duty, U.S. Navy, 1998–2005
Assignment: Research Scientist, Naval Medical Research and Development Command, Bethesda, MD

- Duties: conducted research on new approaches to combat casualty care
- Research interest: preservation of blood components and substitutes; development of blood component substitutes
- Accomplishments: made substantial progress in developing new, effective blood component substitutes

PUBLICATIONS
Articles in more than 10 publications including several in *Cell*, *Hematology*, and other refereed journals

Complete list available

Page 1 of 2

AWARDS/RECOGNITIONS
- Received Outstanding Science Student Award, Virginia Tech class of 1991 (one of only three graduates to receive this award)
- Graduated summa cum laude from Virginia Tech
- Received Rawlings Fellowship, University of Virginia
- Named Outstanding Young Woman of America, 2002
- Received several Navy awards along with excellent evaluations

VOLUNTEER WORK
- Active in "Big Sister" program, Bethesda, MD
- Volunteer, Special Olympics, Blacksburg, VA

REFERENCES ON REQUEST

ROBERT C. PEREZ

Apartment 4-B
Anderson Ridge Apartments
3400 Bryant Avenue
Worcester, MA 01608
(508) 555-1486
robertperez@xxx.com

Career Objective

A position where I can use my mechanical skills and aptitudes.

Occupational Accomplishments

- Served in the United States Navy as a Boiler Technician.
- Operated and performed maintenance on boilers, pumps, and related machinery.
- Advanced to Boiler Technician First Class.
- Developed a wide range of mechanical and operational skills.

Military Service Board

Active Duty, 1995–2001
Served aboard U.S.S. John C. Stennis
U.S. Navy Reserve, 2001–Present
Complete service record available on request.

Educational Background

Graduate, Service School Command, Great Lakes, IL.
Completed courses on performing preventive and corrective maintenance on steam-propulsion systems and components.

References

Provided on request.

ROGER E. NUNN

707 Washington Terrace
Concord, NH 03301
(603) 555-2152
roger-nunn@xxx.com

CAREER OBJECTIVE
To obtain a position in machining, machine tool technology, or related field.

EDUCATION
A.S. degree, New Hampshire Vocational-Technical College, Manchester, NH, 1996. Emphasis area: machine tool technology.

- Additional education through U.S. Army training courses.
- Subjects covered included personnel supervision, records management, and organizational management.

RELATED EXPERIENCE
Allied Trades Technician, U.S. Army, 1997 - 2005
Machinist, U.S. Army, 1995 - 1997
Rank at end of Army service: Chief Warrant Officer

- Set up and operated machine tools.
- Made and repaired metal parts, mechanisms, and machinery.
- Supervised subordinates in setting up and using equipment.
- Managed shop operations.
- Interpreted regulations and orders.
- Performed comprehensive duties requiring firsthand knowledge of metalworking techniques and practices, as well as effective supervisory techniques.

SPECIAL ACCOMPLISHMENTS
- Contributed to several issues of *Preventive Maintenance Monthly*, 1995 - 1998.
- Selected to serve on special review team for revision of technical manuals, 1999.

REFERENCES PROVIDED ON REQUEST

ALLEN P. OLESSI

21 Ball Terrace
Spartanburg, SC 29303
(803) 555-4088
allenolessi@xxx.com

SUMMARY OF QUALIFICATIONS

Highly skilled manager experienced in providing leadership for complex, demanding operations. Experienced through service as officer in United States Navy in various aspects of planning, managing, motivating, evaluating, and implementing action plans. Decisive, energetic supervisor.

ACCOMPLISHMENTS

Recently completed a highly successful 20-year career with the United States Navy. Served in several highly important roles, including Executive Officer of an aircraft carrier with a crew of more than 5,000.

PROFESSIONAL EXPERIENCE

U.S. Navy, 1982–2004

Began career as an Ensign assigned to U.S.S. *Tarawa*. Also served on U.S.S. *Virginia*, U.S.S. *Forrestal*, and U.S.S. *Nimitz*, where I served as Executive Officer. Reached rank of Commander. Received numerous commendations and recognitions for service.

Complete military record available on request.

EDUCATION

M.S. in Management
Virginia State University, Petersburg, VA, 1994

B.S. in Business Management with a minor in Military Science
Georgia Institute of Technology, Atlanta, GA, 1989
GPA: 3.4
Member, Naval R.O.T.C.

Additional training obtained through various Navy courses.

REFERENCES PROVIDED ON REQUEST

BRIAN PAINTER

507 Sunnyview Place • Boulder, Colorado 80306
(303) 555-4557 • brian.painter@xxx.com

CAREER OBJECTIVE
To obtain a position requiring excellent organizational and leadership skills.

MILITARY SERVICE/PROFESSIONAL EXPERIENCE
2003–2005
Fleet Marine Force, Atlantic
Norfolk, Virginia
Rank: Captain

1998–2003
First Marine Amphibious Force
Camp Pendleton, California
Rank: First Lieutenant (promoted from Second Lieutenant, 1997)

1994–1998
Student member, Reserve Officer Training Corps (R.O.T.C.)
University of Colorado, Boulder, Colorado

DUTIES/SKILLS
In all positions as Marine Corps officer, provided key role in training, preparing, and leading combat-ready troops.

Specialized in amphibious operations. Duties required assertiveness, mental and physical vigor, highly developed leadership qualities, loyalty, and excellent skills in planning, organizing, and managing.

EDUCATION
Bachelor of Science, University of Colorado, 1998
Major: Business Management
Minor: Marketing

Twenty-four credits toward master's degree, Old Dominion University, Norfolk, Virginia

REFERENCES PROVIDED ON REQUEST

CHRISTOPHER PASCOE

21 Lake Avenue Circle
Palos Heights, Illinois 60463
(708) 555-4376 (voice)
(708) 555-6062 (fax)
christopherpascoe@xxx.com

SUMMARY OF QUALIFICATIONS

- Experienced, highly competent plumber and pipe fitter
- Developed and applied plumbing skills while on active duty in United States Army
- Reliable worker
- Skilled at working productively and efficiently

WORK EXPERIENCE

Plumber, United States Army: 1993 - 2005
Duties: Performed basic plumbing services, including installation and maintenance
Rank: Sergeant
Performance level: Received various service awards and recognitions (complete military record available)

Laborer, United Cities Construction, Palos Heights, Illinois: Summers, 1989 - 1993

EDUCATION

Graduate, Engineer School, Fort Leonard Wood, Missouri, 1989
(Plumbing Course 720-51KIO)

REFERENCES

Available on request

Masha Mahaffey

2144 Falconer Highway
Louisville, KY 40232
(502) 555-0496
masha_mahaffey@xxx.com

Summary of Qualifications

Expert, experienced technician trained in maintaining, servicing, and repairing radio equipment.

Professional Experience

1998–2005 United States Navy
Position: Electronics Technician First Class
Specialty: Radio equipment maintenance and repair

Responsibilities:
- Performed comprehensive services in installing, maintaining, and repairing radio equipment.
- Read and interpreted schematics.
- Used a variety of tools and equipment.
- Performed troubleshooting functions.
- Prepared preventive-maintenance schedules.
- Maintained parts inventory.
- Performed other related duties.

Education/Training

Graduate, Service School Command, San Diego, CA, 1998
- Completed Navy training courses in basic electronics, AC and DC circuits, electronic instrumentation, radio set maintenance, and related subjects.
- Familiar with and comfortable using Microsoft and Mac operating systems.
- Skilled in using MS Office and Lotus Notes.

References

Reference information provided on request.

MARILYN H. MACAULEY

Until June 1, 2005
910 Collins Street
Burlington, VT 05401
(207) 555-4404

After June 1, 2005
277 Fairview Extension
Apartment 6B
Portland, ME 04101
(802) 555-7137

EDUCATIONAL BACKGROUND

Associate in Applied Science (Engineering Technology), Trident Technical College, Charleston, SC, 1998.

Twelve semester hours at University of South Carolina (Engineering and Business).

Naval training courses completed in a variety of areas including:
• Basic aircraft maintenance.
• Aircraft jet engine maintenance.
• Propeller, fuel, and exhaust systems maintenance.
• Basic helicopter drive system maintenance.
• Aircraft maintenance management.
• Personnel administration.

WORK EXPERIENCE

Chief Aviation Machinists' Mate (E-7), U.S. Navy.
Left military service voluntarily to return to civilian life, 2002.
Stationed at Charleston Naval Base, Charleston, SC.
• Took on increasing levels of responsibility and gained expertise, serving as Airman, Aviation Machinists' Mate, Third Class, Second Class, and First Class.
• Mastered comprehensive array of skills involved in maintaining aircraft engines and related systems. Became thoroughly familiar with induction, cooling, fuel, oil, compression, combustion, turbine, and exhaust systems.

Page 1 of 2

WORK EXPERIENCE *(CONTINUED)*

- Conducted a wide range of service and repair tasks.
- Performed management role that included supervising work groups and completing tasks related to planning and management.

SPECIAL SKILLS

- Highly skilled at performing complex tasks needed to provide safe, efficient service, maintenance, and repair of aircraft.
- Experienced in supervising others and managing the planning and execution of maintenance and repair functions.

REFERENCES AVAILABLE ON REQUEST

Michael Melendez
3350 Brookside Avenue
Salem, OR 97309
(503) 555-2381
michaelmelendez@xxx.com

Objective: A challenging position in the food service industry

Education: A.A.S., Seattle Community College, 1999
                      Major: Food Service Management

                      Additional training through U.S. Army

Work Experience: Served as Food Service Technician, U. S. Army
                      Rank: Warrant Officer, 1992–2005

Experience: Fifteen years' highly successful performance, receiving
                      consistently high evaluations from superior officers

                      Performed the following duties:
                      • Supervised and administered comprehensive food
                        service activities for large military installation
                      • Maintained operational control over personnel,
                        facilities, and equipment
                      • Supervised procurement, storage, distribution, and
                        preparation of foods
                      • Performed wide range of duties with emphasis on
                        technical and human resource areas of food service
                        administration
                      • Exercised both reliability in carrying out policies and
                        directives and creativity in enhancing various aspects
                        of food preparation, service, and overall management

Memberships: National Food Service Association
                      Optimists International

References: Provided on request

SARAH KABULSKI-LONG

1305 Glade Spring Circle
Santa Cruz, CA 95064
(408) 555-3323
sarah-kabulskilong@xxx.com

EMPLOYMENT OBJECTIVE

To obtain a position in computer-support services utilizing my training in computer programming

RELATED SKILLS AND EXPERIENCE

- Experienced in writing, analyzing, testing, and implementing computer programs
- Competent in COBOL, C++, BASIC, Pascal, RPG, ILE, IFS, XML, CL, SQL, and Web page design, setup, and maintenance
- Experienced in conducting data-systems studies involving investigation, evaluation, development, and implementation of new and modified data-processing systems
- Skilled in applying advanced programming techniques

WORK BACKGROUND

Programmer/Analyst, United States Army, 1999–2005
Computer/Machine Operator, United States Army, 1995–1999

TRAINING/EDUCATION

Bachelor of Science, University of the Pacific, 2005
Major: Computer Science
Minor: Mathematics

Completed Army training courses at Information Systems Software Center, Fort Belvoir, VA

REFERENCES WILL BE PROVIDED ON REQUEST

SUSAN A. LOMBARDO

21 Lake Avenue Circle • Palos Heights, Illinois 60463
(708) 555-4376 (voice) • (708) 555-6062 (fax)
susanlombardo@xxx.com

SUMMARY OF QUALIFICATIONS

- Experienced military police officer.
- Highly trained and experienced in performing basic law-enforcement duties.
- Dependable, levelheaded, and energetic.
- Adept at using good judgment in a wide range of settings and situations.

WORK EXPERIENCE

United States Army, 1997–2005
Role: Military Police Officer
Duties: Performed a wide range of duties. Experience included base security, routine and special patrols, traffic management, and assisting in criminal investigations.

EDUCATION

- Graduate of Military Police School, Fort McClellan, Alabama.
- Completed additional courses in criminal investigation methods, Fort Gordon, Georgia.
- High school graduate with six college credits through dual-enrollment program (English Composition and American History).

TECHNICAL SKILLS

Highly skilled in a wide range of law-enforcement skills including crowd control, appropriate weapons use, and arrest procedures.

REFERENCES

Personal and professional references available on request.

CARTER KATZ

474 East Triangle Street

Adrian, MI 49221

(517) 555-2686

carterkatz@xxx.com

CAREER OBJECTIVE
A position in mail room management or related field

EXPERIENCE
Postal Specialist, United States Army, 2000–2005
- Performed a variety of duties involved in processing domestic and international mail
- Requisitioned, safeguarded, and issued stamps, money orders, supplies, and equipment
- Maintained and audited postal accounts
- Operated and supervised postal service center and integrated retail terminals

Package Handler, United Parcel Service, 1999–2000
- Loaded and unloaded trucks; performed miscellaneous duties as part-time, temporary employee

EDUCATION AND TRAINING
- Completed Postal Supervisor Course, Soldier Support Center, Fort Benjamin Harrison, IN, 2000
- Additional studies completed through correspondence and other Army training in personnel management and accounting
- Diploma, South High School, Minneapolis, MN

SPECIAL SKILLS/KNOWLEDGE
Familiar with a variety of equipment including:
- Manual and automated postage meters
- Postage scales
- Electronic mail-sorting equipment
- Bar code printers and readers

REFERENCES AVAILABLE ON REQUEST

JUDY L. CHANG

500 South Parkway, Apartment 19
Muncie, Indiana 47306
(317) 555-3316 (home)
(317) 555-9745 (cellular)
judychang@xxx.com

OBJECTIVE
A position in secretarial support, administration, or marketing.

EXPERIENCE
2000 - 2005
Administrative Specialist, United States Army.

- ❖ Served as executive administrative assistant.
- ❖ Typed and word processed documents using Microsoft Word.
- ❖ Prepared correspondence and reports.
- ❖ Filed records and coordinated filing systems.
- ❖ Provided general administrative support.
- ❖ Promoted from administrative clerk, providing basic office-support functions.

SKILLS
- ❖ Possess excellent written/verbal communication skills with the ability to handle multiple tasks in a fast-paced environment.
- ❖ Proficient in computer skills including Word, Excel, PowerPoint, and Access.
- ❖ Type 55 words per minute.
- ❖ Familiar with multiple database programs including ACT!
- ❖ Comfortable with learning new technology.

EDUCATION
Graduate, Adjutant General School, Soldier Support Institute.
Fort Benjamin Harrison, Indiana, 2004.
Completed Administrative Specialist course (self-paced).

Administration School, Fort Jackson, South Carolina.
Six credits in Secretarial Science, 2000.

Indiana Vocational-Technical College, Indianapolis, Indiana.

REFERENCES
Available on request.

• Latasha Hughes Jones •

**2120 Fairview Avenue
Columbus, Ohio 43216
(614) 555-1508
latasha-jones@xxx.com**

• Career Goal
A position in emergency services, comprehensive health care, or other health-care service

• Experience
• Six years of active service in the United States Navy (1999–2005)
• Served most recently as Hospital Corpsman First Class

• Assignments
Meridian Naval Air Station, Meridian, Mississippi
Guantanamo Bay Naval Station, Cuba

• Professional Specialty
Emergency services
Experience performing Pulmonary Function Test
Respirator-fit testing
Great interpersonal skills
Great communication skills

• Education
• A.D.N. Cuyahoga Community College, Cleveland, Ohio, 1999
• Completed additional United States Navy training in records and information management, personnel supervision, and facilities management (Great Lakes Naval Training Center)

• Memberships
American Nursing Association

References Available on Request

Jamal V. Johnson

4900 Ridgeway Place • El Paso, TX 79968

(401) 555-1895 Home • (401) 555-6564 Cellular

jamal_johnson@xxx.com

PROFESSIONAL OBJECTIVE

Seeking a position in the civilian health-care field utilizing my skills and experience in physical therapy.

EXPERIENCE

1995–2005 Physical Therapy Specialist, United States Army
Rank: Staff Sergeant
- Performed comprehensive duties in physical therapy treatment and exercises.
- Utilized various techniques including heat, ice, ultrasound, hydrotherapy, massage, electrical stimulation, and manual exercise procedures.
- Prepared patient and administrative reports.
- Assisted in clinic management.

EDUCATION

- Graduate, Academy of Health Sciences, Fort Sam Houston, TX, 1995.
- Completed both Phase I (17 weeks) and Phase II (10 weeks) in physical therapy techniques.
- Completed additional continuing-education courses, 1999 and 2005.

REFERENCES

References available on request.

Shawna A. Jefferson
238 Heather Avenue
Sioux City, Iowa 51104
(712) 555-0960 Home
(712) 555-7430 Cellular
shawnajefferson@xxx.com

Career Objective

A position providing paralegal assistance in a progressive law practice

Achievements and Experience

Served as a Senior Chief Legalman (E-8) in the United States Navy, 1994–2003
In this capacity, performed the following:

- Fulfilled a wide range of paralegal duties under the supervision of legal officers
- Assisted in preparing legal research using references including federal and state codes, legal encyclopedias, legal digests, and online resources
- Coordinated office functions in judge advocate's office
- Reviewed records and reports for accuracy and legal adequacy
- Prepared records and documents using computers, stenotype machines, and other office equipment
- Assisted personnel in obtaining legal services
- Earned outstanding performance ratings

Skills

- Ability to read and comment on documents thoroughly to determine accuracy of information
- Excellent written and oral communications skills
- Strong organizational skills
- Ability to work independently and pay close attention to details
- Ability to work in a fast-paced environment
- High degree of independent analysis and judgment

Education

Graduate, Naval Justice School, Newport, Rhode Island, 1999
Associate of Arts, Miami-Dade Community College, Miami, Florida, 1996

Memberships

American Paralegal Society
Civitans

References

Available on request

✚ Denise Jackson-Smith

906 Fair Meadow Street
Dayton, OH 45469
(513) 555-9765
denise.jacksonsmith@xxx.com

Employment Objective

Obtain a position in maintaining, servicing, and repairing medical equipment

Professional Experience

1999–2005 United States Army
Position: Medical Equipment Repairer, Unit Level

Responsibilities:
Provided a wide range of service and repairs for a variety of medical equipment, including the following types:

✚ Mechanical   ✚ Electronic
✚ Hydraulic   ✚ Digital
✚ Gas   ✚ Solid-state
✚ Steam   ✚ Radiological
✚ Electrical   ✚ Optical

Duties included the following:
✚ Performed routine maintenance, service, calibration, and repair of medical equipment
✚ Inspected, inventoried, and assembled new equipment
✚ Serviced and repaired equipment including pulmonary equipment, monitoring systems, diathermy systems, spectrophotometers, ultrasonic equipment, anesthesia apparatus, operating tables, and other systems and individual units

Training

Completed Army training courses in solid-state electronics, AC circuits, DC circuits, electronic instrumentation, pneumatic and hydraulic controls, mechanical and electromechanical controls, electronic equipment diagnostics and repair, and related subjects

References

Complete reference information will be made available on request.

Charles H. Ingram

Route 4, Box 112
Isleboro, Maine 04848
(207) 555-1219
CHARLESINGRAM@XXX.COM

Summary of Qualifications
- Energetic, highly motivated team player experienced in working with others to achieve common goals
- Physically fit and mentally vigorous
- Available to take on new challenges following successful period of military service

Experience
1999 - 2005 United States Navy
Rating: Mineman First Class (E-6)
- Maintained, installed, and inspected underwater explosive devices
- Instructed junior personnel in handling explosives and detonation agents
- Supervised handling, assembling, disassembling, testing, and storage of mines
- Prepared mine cases and other components for assembly
- Used a wide variety of tools and testing devices
- Performed other related duties requiring diligence, concentration, and adherence to safety

1998 - 1999 Stocker, Cook's Grocery, Isleboro, Maine
- Performed general store duties while employed on part-time basis

Education
Graduate, Fleet and Mine Warfare Training Center
Charleston, South Carolina, 2000

Diploma, Isleboro High School
Isleboro, Maine, 1999

References
Available on request

Rachel E. Huan

275 Rolling Hills Drive
Toms River, New Jersey 08753
(201) 555-6622 home
(201) 555-8890 cellular phone
rachelhuan@xxx.com

Objective
A challenging position in the printing industry.

Work Background
2001–2005
Printing and Binding Specialist, U.S. Army.

1999–2001
Infantryman, U.S. Army.

1997–1999
Office Assistant, Hollings Publications, Toms River, New Jersey.

Printing Experience/Skills
Through Army experience and training, became thoroughly proficient in operating offset presses, bindery equipment, and duplication equipment. This included supervising photolithographic activities as well as performing direct printing and binding tasks.

Possess IBM, HP, Lexmark, Epson, OKI, and OEM printer-maintenance certifications.

Education
Completed several U.S. Army training courses.
Graduate, Fairview High School, Fairview, New Jersey.

Special Recognitions
Received commendations for outstanding performance, including good conduct medal and excellent evaluations from superiors.

References available on request

DOUG HINES

526 Calhoun Street • Silver City, NM 88062
(505) 555-4448 • douglashines@xxx.com

JOB OBJECTIVE

To obtain a position utilizing my skill and
background as a trained researcher.

WORK EXPERIENCE

1998–2005 Biological Sciences Assistant, United States Army.
Duties: Performed professional-level laboratory and research duties in
biological science. Conducted studies as part of Army research projects—
some projects classified; specialized in small-animal nervous systems as
affected by toxins.

1996–1998 Graduate Research Assistant, University of New Mexico.
Duties: Performed general laboratory duties under faculty supervision.

SPECIAL SKILLS/INTERESTS

- Skilled in use of computers and related applications in research
  methodologies.
- Possess working knowledge of German.

PUBLICATIONS

Author or coauthor of several publications; complete list and/or copies of
articles available on request.

EDUCATION

M.S., University of New Mexico, 2000.
Major: Biology
- Thesis: "Effects of Pesticides on Amphibian Desert Populations"

B.S., University of New Mexico, 1998.
Major: Biology
Minor: Chemistry
- Graduated magna cum laude.
- Member, Alpha Mu Kappa Honorary Science Society.
- Dean's List eight semesters.

MEMBERSHIP

American Biology Association

References are available on request.

LISA M. HENRY

532 Monitor Drive
Columbus, OH 43215
(614) 555-3987
lisahenry@xxx.com

PROFESSIONAL EXPERIENCE

2003–2005	Photography Warrant Officer, U.S. Navy
2000–2003	Photographer's Mate, U.S. Navy
1998–2000	Darkroom Assistant, Connor Photography, Columbus, OH (part-time and summers)

EDUCATION

Graduate, Advanced Photography Training Course, School of Photography
Corry Station, Pensacola, FL, 2003

College courses completed in photography, technical writing, and general studies
(24 credit hours completed toward bachelor's degree)
Virginia Commonwealth University, Richmond, VA

Completed several additional Navy training courses
(completion certificates and/or transcripts available on request)

SPECIAL SKILLS

• Photographic lab techniques
• Lab supervision
• Color photography
• Illustrative photography
• Aerial photography
• Photojournalism
• Portraiture
• Color correction
• Photoshop and Illustrator

REFERENCES ON REQUEST

Brian Hawkins

108-B North Madison
College Station, Texas 77843
(409) 555-1245
brianhawkins@xxx.com

Employment Objective
Position as an air traffic controller or related position in aviation operation or management

Experience
➤ Fifteen years of experience with the U.S. Army (1990–2005), including twelve years of active service as an ATC operator
➤ Experienced with Visual Flight Rules (VFR), Special Visual Flight Rules (SVFR), and Instrument Flight Rules (IFR)
➤ Provided radar and nonradar air traffic control services
➤ Provided flight control for takeoffs, flights, and landings for military and civilian aircraft
➤ Performed with excellence and reliability

Education
Completed ATC training at Aviation Center
Fort Rucker, Alabama, 1992

Membership
Association of Air Traffic Controllers

References
References and additional background information, including transcripts, available on request

Tawnya A. Groves

3200 Old Farm Road
Kearney, NE 68849
Home: (308) 555-0409
Cell: (308) 555-6618
tawnyagroves@xxx.com

JOB OBJECTIVE

To obtain a position in inventory, logistics management, or another related field

EDUCATION

University of Maryland, College Park, MD
Completed 40 semester hours in Business Administration

Quartermaster School, Fort Lee, VA
Completed several special trainings on property accounting/management

WORK EXPERIENCE

1999–2005: Property Accounting Technician, U.S. Navy
Rank: Warrant Officer
Duties:
- Performed comprehensive duties related to property accountability
- Managed property books, both manual and automated
- Utilized appropriate accounting procedures
- Planned supply requirements and completed forecasts
- Established procedures for obtaining, storing, and issuing supplies
- Prepared reports and correspondence
- Completed additional related duties
- Advanced through promotion from previous position of Unit Supply Specialist

1997–1999: Child Care Worker, Tots, Inc., Kearney, NE

SPECIAL SKILLS/INTERESTS
- Skilled in use of computers
- Conversant in American Sign Language (ASL)
- Volunteer interpreter for the deaf

MEMBERSHIPS
- American Logistics Association
- Nebraska Interpreters League

REFERENCES PROVIDED ON REQUEST

ALLISON GOSNEY

206 Jeffries Drive
Riverdale, NY 10471
(212) 555-2013
a.gosney@xxx.com

EMPLOYMENT OBJECTIVE

To obtain a challenging position in the airline industry

RELATED SKILLS AND EXPERIENCE

- Experienced in various aspects of providing service for air passengers
- Skilled in all steps required for processing passenger reservations
- Thoroughly familiar with automated data-processing functions for passenger reservations
- Experienced in developing positive relations with customers and maintaining good customer relations
- Highly motivated self-starter interested in taking on new challenges
- Familiar with current airline codes and laws
- Fluent in Spanish

WORK BACKGROUND

1998–2005
Air Passenger Specialist, United States Air Force
- Completed special job-related training by correspondence through Air Force Extension Course Institute, Gunter Air Force Base, AL
- Received excellent evaluations of job performance

REFERENCES

Complete reference information and military record provided on request

JOSHUA GOLDSTEIN

205 Pendleton Street, Apt. 16-B ◆ Americus, Georgia 31709
(912) 555-2918 ◆ joshuagoldstein@xxx.com

CAREER OBJECTIVE

To obtain a position in service and repair of electronic data equipment

EDUCATION

Associate of Applied Science in Computer Electronics, Greenville Technical College, Greenville, South Carolina, 1999

Additional training through U.S. Navy training courses at Combat Systems Technical School, Mare Island, California, 2000–2001

RELATED EXPERIENCE

◆ Served as Data Technician First Class, U.S. Navy
◆ Performed general maintenance and repairs on computers, data link devices, and other electronic data equipment
◆ Inspected and tested equipment and components
◆ Diagnosed and repaired malfunctions in computers, data-storage devices, and other equipment
◆ Performed troubleshooting and adjustment of electromechanical devices in digital systems
◆ Prepared maintenance schedules for electronic data equipment
◆ Effectively utilized various hand tools and electronic equipment

SPECIAL SKILLS/MEMBERSHIPS

◆ Highly skilled in troubleshooting process
◆ Member, Professional Electronic Technicians Association (ETA)
◆ Currently undergoing ETA certification process

REFERENCES PROVIDED ON REQUEST

PATRICIA G. FRANKS

335 Canyon Drive • Bozeman, MT 59717
(406) 555-3490 • patriciafranks@xxx.com

EDUCATION

Montana State University, School of Business, Bozeman, MT
Bachelor of Science in Business Administration, 2004
Concentration: Finance and Accounting

ACTIVITIES AND AWARDS

• Accounting Club
• Dean's List
• Letter of Appreciation, U.S. Marine Corps

EMPLOYMENT

Jones & Parker, Bozeman, MT, January 2004 to July 2004
Salesperson and Cashier, part-time
  • Assisted customers and oversaw cash register procedures

Mountain Radio Group, Bozeman, MT, April 2002 to November 2003
Corporate Bookkeeper
  • Reconciled monthly bank statements
  • Prepared monthly financial statements and bimonthly payroll for five
    stations
  • Managed accounts receivable and payable

Quality Heating Co., Billings, MT, February 2001 to April 2002
Bookkeeper
  • Prepared quarterly tax reports and bimonthly payroll
  • Managed accounts receivable and payable

Jobs Unlimited, Boise, ID, December 1999 to January 2001
Credit Assistant
  • Performed credit checks for new accounts
  • Managed accounts receivable

U.S. Marine Corps, January 1994 to December 1999
Corporal

REFERENCES AVAILABLE

John R. Fleming Jr.

4215 Pilot Creek Road
Clinton, MS 39058
(601) 555-7228
john-fleming@xxx.com

Career Objective

A position in aviation mechanics or a related field.

Work Experience

- Served as Gunnery Sergeant (E-7), United States Marine Corps.
- Completed 12 years of active service concluding July 2005.
- Performed highest level of tasks (Level 4) in helicopter maintenance and repair.
- Planned and scheduled activities of aircraft maintenance work centers.
- Performed a wide range of inspection and maintenance duties, including performing aviation unit (AVUM), intermediate (AVIM), and depot maintenance on aircraft electrical systems, power train systems, aircraft turbine engines and components, structures, pneudraulics systems, aviation communications, navigation, identification friend or foe (IFF), radar, and flight-control equipment.

Training and Education

- Certificate, Aircraft Maintenance, Lansing Technical College, Lansing, MI, 1993.
- Completed Marine Training courses in aviation mechanics (Air Ground Combat Center, Twentynine Palms, CA), 1998 and 2001, and in personnel management (correspondence), 2004.

References Available

ROBERT A. FIGUEROA

2175 Broadway • Morganton, North Carolina 28655
(704) 555-3795 • (704) 555-0908 cell phone
rob-figueroa@xxx.com

OBJECTIVE

A senior management position requiring leadership, decisiveness, and vision.

PROFESSIONAL BACKGROUND

Career military officer, United States Army
Active service: June 1986–present
Rank: Major General

CAREER SUMMARY:

- Began service as a Second Lieutenant.
- Served as a combat infantry officer in South Korea.
- Progressed through officer ranks with consistently high evaluations.
- In addition to Korea, stationed in West Germany, Afghanistan, and several postings in the continental United States, including the Pentagon.
- Specialized in infantry leadership with secondary specialty in tactical/strategic intelligence.

AWARDS/ACCOMPLISHMENTS

- Received numerous medals, ribbons, and other recognitions including Bronze Star, Purple Heart, Meritorious Service Medal, and others.
- Consistently earned praise from superior officers for outstanding performance.

EDUCATION

M.B.A., University of Texas, Austin, Texas, 1994.
Completed additional studies at U.S. Army Command and General Staff College, Fort Leavenworth, Kansas, and at Army War College, Carlisle Barracks, Pennsylvania.

B.S., United States Military Academy, West Point, New York, 1986.
- Graduated in top 25 percent of class.

Additional details regarding Army career available on request.

References provided on request.

RICARDO ESTEBAN

105 Upland Drive
Sanford, FL 32773
(407) 555-4103
ricardoesteban@xxx.com

Career Objective

Responsible position utilizing my education and background as an experienced veterinarian

Professional History

Veterinarian, United States Army: 1994–2005
- ❯ Researched animal diseases
- ❯ Inspected food to determine condition and quality
- ❯ Inspected cleanliness of facilities for food processing, meat packaging, and food storage
- ❯ Planned measures for controlling contagious diseases transmitted by animals or food

Veterinary Technician, White Animal Hospital, Tallahassee, FL: part-time and summers 1990–1994
Performed basic support services including
- ❯ Assisting in animal care
- ❯ Doing kennel maintenance
- ❯ Providing client support and related tasks

Education and Training

D.V.M., Florida State University, 1994
Special areas of interest: small-animal practice research methodologies

B.S., Florida State University, 1990
Major: Biology
Minor: Physical Science
GPA: 3.8

Memberships

- ❯ American Veterinary Medical Association
- ❯ Florida Association of Veterinary Medicine

References available as requested

Lisa Erdman

398 Berger Street
Medford, OR 97501
(503) 555-8007
Lisa-Erdman@xxx.com

Objective
Position in payroll or other related business operations

Military Work Experience
United States Navy, 1998–2004
Rating: Disbursing Clerk First Class (E-6)

Duties included the following:
- Maintained personnel financial records, including payroll, using Excel spreadsheets and other office software
- Processed travel allowances and reimbursements
- Prepared correspondence and reports
- Processed vouchers for receipt and expenditure of funds
- Applied Navy regulations in computation of pay
- Prepared payroll checks
- Trained and supervised less-experienced personnel
- Coordinated office work flow

Training/Education
Successfully completed courses in the following:
- Microsoft Office Suite (Word, Excel, Access, and PowerPoint)
- Keyboarding
- Office procedures
- Automatic data processing
- Payroll accounting
- Office administration
- Internal auditing
- Principles of supervision

References available on request

SHARON L. DUARTE

760 Hunters Mill Road

Helena, AR 72342

(501) 555-2624

s.duarte@xxx.com

CAREER OBJECTIVE
A challenging role in human resources administration

BACKGROUND
United States Coast Guard, 1990–2005
Job Specialty: Personnel Administration
Rank: Warrant Officer

RELATED SKILLS AND EXPERIENCE
- Performed a wide range of duties in personnel administration and general management
- Advised Coast Guard personnel (both enlisted and officers) regarding personnel regulations and procedures
- Supervised as many as 18 workers in preparing and maintaining a comprehensive array of personnel records and accounts
- Prepared official correspondence and administered directives
- Provided leadership and oversight for various stages of office automation and computerization

SPECIAL SKILLS
- Highly skilled in analyzing policies and procedures and interpreting them for personnel at various skill levels
- Proficient in use of personal computers and LAN (local area network) systems for management purposes
- Skilled in effective communication, both oral and written

TRAINING/EDUCATION
Associate Degree, Trident Technical College
Charleston, SC
Concentration: Business Administration
Additional education through Coast Guard training courses

REFERENCES AVAILABLE ON REQUEST

LINDA DIAZ DAVIS

708 Carson Road
Morganton, NC 28655
(704) 555-3795 Home
(704) 555-0990 Cellular
Linda-Davis@xxx.com

OBJECTIVE

A position in industrial security, hospital security, or a related area.

RELEVANT SKILLS AND EXPERIENCE

- Experienced in various aspects of protecting property and personnel.
- Skilled in performing physical security inspections.
- Familiar with effective procedures for reducing threats, anticipating security problems, and dealing with contemporary security issues.
- Skilled in using fire equipment, weapons, locks, alarms, and other devices and equipment related to security.
- Adept at various self-defense measures.
- Highly reliable in following orders, implementing procedures, and acting independently when needed.

WORK HISTORY

1996–2005 United States Marine Corps
- Completed basic training at Paris Island, SC.
- Served as security guard at military installations, including assignment at United States Embassy in Cairo, Egypt.
- Received several commendations for outstanding service.
- Decided not to reenlist after two tours of duty in favor of a civilian career in security.

EDUCATION

- Graduate, Security Guard School, Quantico, VA, 1996.
- Completed more than 100 hours of language training, specializing in Arabic.
- Fluent in Spanish.
- Completed several correspondence courses and seminars related to security practices and procedures.

REFERENCES ON REQUEST

MARILYN DAUGHERTY

405 Warren Street
Mt. Pleasant, TX 75455
(903) 555-8631
marilyndaugherty@xxx.com

SUMMARY OF QUALIFICATIONS

Highly experienced in maintaining and repairing aircraft electrical, instrument, and power systems. Skilled and well trained in performing with efficiency and diligent attention to safety standards. Also experienced in effective management and supervision.

ACHIEVEMENTS

- Served effectively for a 10-year tour with the United States Navy
- Reached rating of E-7, Chief Aviation Electrician's Mate
- Demonstrated highly developed technical skills
- Worked with a variety of aircraft types
- Received excellent evaluations of performance
- Supervised more than 15 personnel
- Performed a variety of planning, management, and reporting functions

WORK HISTORY

1995–2005
United States Navy
Progressed from Airman to Chief Aviation Electrician's Mate.
Served aboard U.S.S. *America*. Specialized in repair and maintenance of aircraft electrical systems.

1993–1995
Cox Electrical Service, Mt. Pleasant, TX
Electrician's Assistant.

EDUCATION

Certificate, Tidewater Community College, Portsmouth, VA, 1997 (included 18 semester credit hours in electricity/electrical systems).

Completed additional training at Naval Air Technical Training Center, Memphis, TN, 1995 and 2000. Courses covered electrical, electronic, and engine instrument systems; aviation weapons systems; physics; technical mathematics; and related topics.

REFERENCES

Available on request.

• Larry Crowe •

8 Progress Way • Pearl City, HI 96782 • (808) 555-3050
larrycrowe@xxx.com

Summary of Qualifications
- Highly experienced in servicing and repairing aircraft and pneumatic systems.
- Skilled in inspecting, maintaining, and repairing hydraulic/pneumatic systems and systems components.
- Specialized in KC-130 aircraft.

Accomplishments
- Served as Aircraft Hydraulic/Pneumatic Mechanic, United States Marine Corps.
- Received excellent performance ratings. Earned several promotions, progressing to rank of Staff Sergeant (E-6).
- Mastered a variety of tasks related to servicing and repairing aircraft systems based on hydraulic and pneumatic principles.
- Worked with a variety of tools and equipment.
- Read and interpreted schematic diagrams, blueprints, and other diagrams.
- Reached advanced performance level.
- Worked independently.
- Provided supervision and instruction to those under me.

Employment History
Staff Mechanic, 2003–present.
Avis Aviation, Pearl City, HI.

United States Marine Corps, 1995–2003.
Served at several bases with primary assignment at Marine Corps Air Station, Kaneohe Bay, HI.

Education
Graduate, Warren Wilson High School, Lansing, MI.

Successfully completed military training courses including United States Marine Corps correspondence course 13.45, Hydraulic Principles and Troubleshooting, offered by Marine Corps Institute, Washington, D.C.

References Provided on Request.

Linda T. Combs
Public Relations Specialist

1906 First Street
Coast Mesa Beach, California 92626
(714) 555-3408
LindaCombs@xxx.com

Summary of Qualifications

❖ Energetic, articulate public relations professional.
❖ Skilled in all aspects of writing, designing, editing, and producing publications.
❖ Experienced in writing news releases, print ads, newsletters, and other material.

Achievements

❖ Developed award-winning series of publications on career opportunities offered by U.S. Coast Guard (Gold Medal Award, California Public Relations Society).
❖ Completed writing, design, and layout for more than 100 Coast Guard publications.
❖ Initiated expanded community-relations program designed to foster good relations with area businesses and civilian population.
❖ Designed and wrote newsletter for district personnel and their families.
❖ Received Outstanding Communicator Award from Long Beach Chamber of Commerce.

Work History

1999–2004
Public Affairs Officer, United States Coast Guard, Fifth Coast Guard District, Long Beach, California
❖ Performed a wide range of duties related to public information/public relations.
❖ Wrote and designed brochures and other publications.
❖ Wrote news releases, ads, scripts, and other informational materials.
❖ Assisted in planning and implementing public relations/public information campaigns.

1997–1999
Advertising Representative, K & B Media, Long Beach, California

Education

B.S., California State University–Long Beach, 2001
Major: Public Relations
Minor: Journalism
GPA: 4.0 in major; 3.83 overall

A.S., Compton Community College, Compton, California, 1997

Memberships

Public Relations Society of America
California Public Relations Society

References Available on Request

Abdul Hakim

312 Maple Drive
Perkinston, MS 39573
601-555-4785
abdul-hakim@xxx.com

Objective:

A position as an avionics technician with a commercial aviation firm.

Education:

Associate Degree, Community College of the Air Force, 2000.
Additional training through Air Force technical courses.

Professional Experience:

1998 - 2003.
Avionics Specialist, United States Air Force.
Provided technical support for fighter aircraft.

1998 - 2001.
363rd Fighter Wing, Shaw Air Force Base, Sumter, SC.

1996 - 1998.
23rd Fighter Wing, England Air Force Base, Alexandria, LA.
Provided comprehensive maintenance and repair service for electronic systems and components of military aircraft. Developed familiarity with instrument systems, electronic warfare equipment, and other systems.

Performance:

Consistently received good or excellent evaluations.
Helped achieve unit commendation award.
Fully eligible for reenlistment but now prefer civilian career.

Complete military record and references are available on request.

Angela Caruso

1501 Welisford Street
Minneapolis, MN 55455
(612) 555-1373
angela.caruso@xxx.com

Education and Training	Certificate in Office Systems Technology Des Moines Area Community College, Des Moines, IA, 1998
	Additional training through completion of military courses and seminars
Professional Experience	1998–2005, Administrative Clerk, United States Marine Corps
	Provided comprehensive clerical support services while serving as enlisted personnel in Marines, stationed at Camp Lejeune, NC
	Performed various duties including the following: • Typed correspondence using MS Word • Maintained correspondence filing system using MS Excel • Prepared documents including fitness reports, leave authorizations, and identification cards • Performed other clerical duties, including mail merges, database maintenance, and phone answering
Special Skills	• Skilled in operating various types of office equipment • Adept in using contemporary word-processing software, including Microsoft Word
References	Available on request

David P. Carleton

1404 Hays Avenue
West Hartford, Connecticut 06117
(203) 555-7565 voice
(203) 555-9343 pager/message
davidcarleton@xxx.com

Summary of Experience

- Ten years' experience in the United States Navy.
- Highly competent data-processing expert.
- Knowledgeable and experienced in all aspects of data processing and information management.

Employment History

U.S. Navy, 1995–2005
Position: Data Processing Limited Duty Officer
Rank: Lieutenant Commander

Service Summary:

- Progressed from Data Processing Warrant Officer to Lieutenant.
- Achieved Commander rank.
- Served as officer technical specialist. Performed bulk of service at Norfolk Naval Station, Norfolk, Virginia.

Duties:

- Performed a wide range of duties in providing electronic data-processing services and supervising such functions.
- Placed emphasis on database management with daily upkeep of the Oracle and TIMSS systems.

Education

Bachelor of Science, North Carolina State University, Raleigh, North Carolina, 1995
Major: Computer Science

Additional training through Navy training courses, including courses on management and supervision

References

Available on request

ann marie brown

3000 Old South Highway, Apartment 6B • Providence, RI 02908
(401) 555-1895 (voice) • (401) 555-2498 (fax)
annmarie-brown@xxx.com

objective

A rewarding position in journalism or public relations

highlights of qualifications

- Fifteen years' experience in writing and editing for the U.S. Army
- A published freelance writer with articles in more than 20 magazines (complete list available on request)
- Experienced in photography as well as written journalism

work experience

1990 - 2005. Journalist, United States Army
- Researched and prepared newspaper articles
- Performed editing and layout duties using PageMaker and Quark
- Coordinated public information activities, including development of news releases
- Trained and supervised subordinates
- Prepared and monitored budgets
- Maintained contacts with representatives of civilian news media

1989 - 1990. Student Editor, *The Daily Progress* (university newspaper)
- Wrote news stories and editorial copy
- Assigned stories to student reporters
- Performed layout and editing duties

education

B.A., Ohio University, Athens, OH, 1990
Major: Journalism.
Minor: Political Science
GPA: 3.2

memberships

- American Society of Journalists and Authors
- National Writers Club

references

Furnished on request

William K. Brown

615 Cardinal Drive
Fergus Falls, MN 56537
(218) 555-0464 (voice)
(218) 555-1855 (fax)
williambrown@xxx.com

Career Objective

A position in surveying or topographic engineering.

Related Skills and Experience

- Highly skilled topographic surveyor with 15 years' experience in the United States Army.
- Achieved advanced skill level through extensive field experience and Army training courses.
- Thoroughly familiar with the most effective contemporary surveying methods, including use of various types of surveying equipment.

Work Background

As Army topographic surveyor, performed tasks such as the following:

- Recorded topographic survey data.
- Operated a variety of survey instruments.
- Performed topographic and geodetic computations.
- Interpreted maps and aerial photographs.
- Performed a wide range of computations including horizontal differences, angular closures, and triangulations.
- Supervised other workers including topographic-instrument-repair specialists.
- Supervised programming of electronic calculators.
- Prepared technical and personnel reports.

Training/Education

Completed military training in mathematics, surveying, engineering computations, technical writing, optics, data processing, and related areas.

References Available on Request

Michael Bleznakov

509 King Street
Evansdale, IN 47713
(812) 555-3618
mike.bleznakov@xxx.com

Education

Bachelor of Arts, University of Kentucky, 1985
Major: English Literature
Minor: Russian

Professional Experience

Intelligence Analyst for United States Army, 1995–2005
Interrogator, United States Army, 1985–1995
Rank: Major

- Performed a wide range of duties requiring strong organizational skills, analytical thinking, and persistence.
- Assembled, integrated, analyzed, and disseminated intelligence information.
- Handled and analyzed information collected from technical, strategic, and tactical sources.
- Supervised receipt, analysis, and storage of intelligence information.
- Compiled, edited, and disseminated intelligence reports.
- Assisted in providing general intelligence training programs.
- Supervised various personnel including interrogators.
- Monitored and interpreted communications via the Internet, e-mail, and phones.

Special Interests

- Fluent in Russian language.
- Efficient with computers and all aspects of their use.
- Highly interested in Eastern European affairs.
- Willing to travel.

References and military record available on request.

JOYCE H. BISHOP

55 Rock Branch Road • Aurora, CO 80045
(303) 555-7954 • joycebishop@xxx.com

SUMMARY OF QUALIFICATIONS
• Experienced medical radiographer.
• Fully licensed and registered.
• Skilled in operating state-of-the-art radiographic equipment.
• Experienced in practicing effective patient relations and interacting with other health-care staff.

ACCOMPLISHMENTS
• Served as active-duty personnel with the United States Army.
• Operated as a valued member of health-care team at two Army medical facilities.
• Received three promotions in rank while on active duty.
• Worked effectively with both military and civilian personnel.

EMPLOYMENT HISTORY
2001–2005, Radiologic Technician
Fitzsimmons Army Medical Center, Aurora, CO 80045
Duties: Utilized x-rays and other ionizing radiation for diagnosis and treatment of medical conditions. Served as technical assistant to radiologists.

1999–2001, Radiologic Technician
Walter Reed Army Medical Canter, Washington, DC 20012

EDUCATION
Associate of Applied Science in Radiography, 1999
Northern Virginia Community College, Annandale, VA

Completed additional courses (nine credit hours in health-care management), 2000–2002
University of Colorado, Boulder, CO

CERTIFICATIONS/MEMBERSHIPS
• Certified (A.S., R.T.) by American Registry of Radiologic Technologists.
• Licensed by Commonwealth of Virginia and State of Colorado; reciprocity in effect for other states.
• Member, American Society of Radiologic Technologists.

REFERENCES
Available on request

James R. Bernstein

29 Appleton Heights
Spokane, WA 99258
(509) 555-0708
jamesbernstein@xxx.com

Employment Objective	A position requiring physical fitness, a strong work ethic, and the ability to work well independently or in combination with others
Experience	2001–2005 United States Army Position: Infantryman Rank: Corporal • Served as an integral member of Army infantry unit • Mastered the use of various weapons including machine guns and antiarmor weapons • Served as team leader, directing deployment and employment of personnel • Performed land navigation • Collected and interpreted intelligence information • Assisted in planning, coordinating, and reporting activities of subordinate units
Education	Diploma, Central High School, Spokane, WA, 2001

Additional education obtained through Army training

References available on request

MOHAMED BEHARI

11805 Boxwood Drive
Costa Mesa, California 92626
(714) 555-4160 (Home)
(714) 555-8764 (Cellular)
mohamed-behari@xxx.com

CAREER GOAL

A rewarding position in dental technology

PROFESSIONAL BACKGROUND

Dental Laboratory Technologist, United States Navy
Date of Service: September 2000 - January 2005

Performed comprehensive duties related to dental fabrication including the following:
- Fabricated basic dental prosthetic devices
- Assembled complete dentures, removable partial dentures, and fixed partial dentures
- Assisted in dental laboratory management
- Maintained inventory of equipment and supplies
- Completed administrative reports
- Implemented and coordinated quality-control measures

EDUCATION/TRAINING

Graduate, U.S. Navy School of Dental Assisting and Technology
San Diego, California, 2000

Additional U.S. Navy courses completed in personnel management

Secondary School Diploma, The Carson School
Los Angeles, California, June 1999

REFERENCES

Provided on request

CHARLES C. BECKMAN

1126 McGill Avenue, Apartment 13-B
Reno, Nevada 89557
Phone (702) 555-6719
Fax (702) 555-7629
charlesbeckman@xxx.com

EDUCATION AND TRAINING

Associate of Arts, Reno Community College, Reno, Nevada (General Studies)

Additional training through completion of Army courses and seminars, including language training

PROFESSIONAL EXPERIENCE

Attaché Technician, United States Army
Rating: Chief Warrant Officer
Embassy Assignment: U.S. Embassy, Caracas, Venezuela

Duties: Provided general administrative and logistical functions in support of Defense Army Attaché office located in U.S. embassy
• Managed and operated logistical support services
• Secured and managed housing for personnel assigned to the embassy
• Advised other personnel regarding protocol and matters of military courtesy
• Supervised enlisted and civilian support specialists
• Managed internal activities of Defense Attaché Office
• Performed other officer-level duties

SPECIAL SKILLS

• Fluent in Spanish
• Skilled in operating personal computers and basic office equipment

REFERENCES

Available on request

Timothy C. Barlow

150 Howell Street • Aden, OK 74820 • (405) 555-2675 • timothybarlow@xxx.com

Objective

Position in warehousing, inventory, or general business where my organizational skills and personal efficiency can assist corporate goals

Achievements and Experience

Served as an Aviation Storekeeper in the United States Navy, 1996–2003

Performed the following duties:
• Received, identified, stored, and issued aviation equipment and supplies
• Conducted inventories and maintained stock-control records
• Used automated data-processing supply procedures
• Maintained receipt-control records
• Prepared various documents including requisitions, financial reports, and inventory records
• Prepared correspondence and messages
• Reviewed computer output for accuracy of records
• Received several promotions in rank, reaching the level of Aviation Storekeeper First Class (E-6)
• Developed a computerized log to record issued equipment, which provided a more accurate way to track status

Special Skills

• Skilled in using a variety of office equipment
• Adept in written and oral communication
• Able to function well under deadlines and other stresses

References and complete military record available on request.

J. DOYLE BAINES

200 N. ELM ST.
BEDFORD, MA 01730
JDOYLEBAINES@XXX.COM

OBJECTIVE:
A position in club management, restaurant management, hotel management, or a related area

EXPERIENCE:
2002–2005, Club Manager, U.S. Army
Officers' Club, Fort Lee, Petersburg, VA
Rank: Warrant Officer

DUTIES:
- Performed a wide range of duties providing day-to-day management of officers' club
- Coordinated purchasing and inventory of supplies
- Coordinated food and beverage services
- Supervised personnel
- Achieved high performance ratings

1999–2002, Assistant Club Manager
Officers' Club, Fort Picket
Blackstone, VA

DUTIES:
- Assisted club manager in all aspects of club management

1997–1999, Waiter
Twin Oaks Restaurant
Bedford, MA

EDUCATION:
Associate of arts degree, J. S. Reynolds Community College, Richmond, VA

Additional training through Army courses including communication skills, food and beverage management, cost-control systems, and personnel management

Also skilled in office-management software, including Microsoft Office

References on request

Ben L. Adkins

151 Badger Street
Janesville, Wisconsin 53547
(608) 555-2402
(608) 555-5645 cell
benadkins@xxx.com

Objective:

Position in service and repair of radio equipment or other electronic equipment

Achievements:

- Served with distinction in United States Army
- Specialized in repair and service of radio equipment
- Military experience included duty under combat conditions (Persian Gulf)
- Developed outstanding skills in identifying and repairing malfunctions

Work History:

1993–2005
Radio Equipment Repairer, United States Army
Served in Second Army, including the following assignments:
- Fort Bragg (Fayetteville, North Carolina)
- Saudi Arabia/Kuwait
- Fort Jackson (Columbia, South Carolina)

Fully trained in the maintenance and repair of radios
Able to troubleshoot and read schematics

1991–1993
Sales Associate, Radio Barn, Janesville, Wisconsin

Education:

Graduate, Signal School, Fort Gordon, Georgia
Diploma, Manning High School, Janesville, Wisconsin
Licensing: Licensed amateur (ham) radio operator

References:

Available on request

Thomas H. Akers

1109 Old Depot Street
Stone Ridge, New York 12484
(914) 555-4124
thomasakers@xxx.com

Summary of Qualifications

- Highly experienced sheet metal worker with seven years' experience in United States Army.
- Adept at using proper techniques for top-quality sheet metal work.
- Highly dependable and productive.

Experience

Served in United States Army, 1994–2005.

Specialized in sheet metal work. Assisted in major projects including base expansion at Fort Lee, Petersburg, Virginia, 1994–1995.

Performed comprehensive duties requiring a broad range of sheet metal construction skills.
These included:
- Fabrication and installation of air ducts.
- Installation of aluminum siding.
- Repair of various structures made of sheet metal.

Education

Diploma, Washington County Vocational-Technical Center, Stone Ridge, New York, 1994.

Additional education through Army training courses.

References

Available on request.

Matthew Slocum

E3 Apple Lane

Kensington, CA 94707

414-555-9085

matthewslocum@xxx.com

Objective:

To obtain a position in Northern California that allows me to use my skills as a Web page designer and HTML programmer

Education:

St. Thomas University, St. Paul, MN

B.A. in Communications and Technology, 2000

Related Experience:

May 2002–present

HTML Programmer, U.S.A. Communications, Oakland, CA

• HTML coder for all Web pages designed by U.S.A. Communications

• Account assistant for three large client Web sites

September 1999–May 2002

Market Researcher, Carey and Associates, St. Paul, MN

• Designed surveys and performed research to support client needs

• Developed a database system for processing research results

July 1998–September 1999

Assistant Editor, *St. Thomas Weekly*

• Assisted in editing, writing, and promoting a student weekly newspaper

• Computerized records and instituted financial reforms resulting in better stability and efficiency for the newspaper

1994–1998

Computer Repair Technician, U.S. Army

• Serviced, installed, and repaired computer systems and related equipment

• Specialized in servicing computers supporting advanced communications equipment

• Received consistently high ratings from superiors

Awards:

• P. E. Lilly Award for Outstanding Academic Achievement
• Dean's List, each of four years of college

Skills:

Programming Languages
  C++
  Cobol
  HTML
  Perl
  MySql
  Java

Software
  Windows XP
  Microsoft Word
  Adobe Acrobat
  Aldus PageMaker
  Adobe Photoshop
  Excel
  Filemaker Pro
  QuarkXPress

Systems
  IBM
  Apple
  UNIX

References Available

Mario Kilde

1267 Buffalo Way • Pleasant Hills, MN 55408 • (612) 555-1232
mariokilde@xxx.com

Objective:	Position as a driver
Summary:	• Ten years' experience in military as a driver of large and small vehicles on base and in city traffic
	• Perfect driving and safety record
	• Familiarity with Twin Cities and surrounding areas
	• Excellent health and personal strength; karate instructor at YMCA
	• Personable, friendly
	• Highly energetic and reliable
	• Proven ability to produce within the confines of a demanding schedule
Other Skills and Experience:	Owner/Manager of Small Business
	• Purchased and delivered retail items, furniture
	• Drove van for merchandise pickup
	• Drove truck for wide variety of short trips in urban areas
	Volunteer Driver, Big Brothers/Big Sisters
	• Drove truck and 15-passenger vans to transport groups of students in hundreds of weekly trips to sporting events and for field trips
	Mail Handler
	• Batched and sorted a large volume of daily mail for dental service company
	• Handled important personal and business mail for clients of QuickMail Etc., including cashing Social Security and disability checks and paying bills
Employment History:	1995–2005 U.S. Army Driver, Fort Snelling, Twin Cities
	1989–1995 Owner/Operator, QuickMail Etc., St. Paul, MN
	1987–1989 Owner/Operator, Gifts and More, Minneapolis, MN
	1985–1987 Mail Handler, Twin City Dental Supply, St. Paul, MN
Education:	Metro State University, 1981–1985
	Coursework: marketing, merchandising, retailing, psychology
	Complete military and employment records and references available on request

Donald B. Davidson

13 Williams Estates   Home: 319-555-2354
Cedar Rapids, Iowa 52406   Mobile: 319-555-9087
donalddavidson@xxx.com

Summary of Qualifications

Experienced in operating a variety of construction equipment and other heavy and light equipment. Highly skilled in earth-moving processes.

Accomplishments

Equipment Operator, active duty, United States Navy
❯ Operated multipurpose excavators and cranes
❯ Operated clamshells, backhoes, pile drivers, and other equipment
❯ Assisted in a variety of construction projects
❯ Advanced from Constructionman (E-3) to Equipment Operator First Class
❯ Earned excellent evaluations from superiors
❯ Held a perfect on-the-job safety record

Employment History

U.S. Navy, 1998–2005
Naval Construction Center
Gulfport, Mississippi

Cook Construction, 1996–1998 (summers)
Cedar Rapids, Iowa

Education

Diploma, South High School, 1996

Completed Navy training courses in equipment operation, safety, and related topics.

References provided on request.

Antonia Harasmus

456 Shady Glade
Pepin, WI 54759
715-555-9898
antoniaharasmus@xxx.com

Employment Objective
To obtain a position in computer support services

Skills and Experience
- Experienced in writing, analyzing, testing, and implementing computer programs
- Competent in a wide variety of computer languages
- Expert inventor of interactive computer games for the adult market
- Qualified to conduct data-systems studies involving meta-analysis techniques
- Skilled in advanced programming techniques
- Fluent in Spanish, including technical terms of the computer industry

Work Background
2002–2005
Programmer/Analyst
United States Army

1999–2002
Video Gaming Consultant
Minnesota Technology Consortium

1996–1999
Youth Adviser to the Governor's Task Force on Youth and Technology
- Appointed by State of Wisconsin Governor Tommy Thompson
- One of two young people asked to serve on task force from 1995 to 1996
- Helped write a proposal to improve computer access for young Wisconsinites through schools and libraries statewide
- Proposal eventually became a bill and was passed in 1997

Training/Education
Bachelor of Science, University of the Pacific, Sacramento, CA, 1996
Major: Computer Science
Minor: Mathematics

Army training courses at Information Systems Software Center,
Fort Belvoir, VA

Volunteer/Travel Experience
- Traveled Latin America after graduation from high school
- Became fluent in Spanish and was trained as a medical aide by
  Catholic Charities in order to assist in emergency posthurricane
  relief work
- Received Medal of Honor from mayor of El Capitan, Peru

Complete military, educational, and employment records are
available at your request.

Kendra Macon

444 West Division Street • Lake Mary, FL 32746
305-555-9032 (home) • 305-555-6743 (cellular)
kendramacon@xxx.com

Objective

Position with local printing press as assistant to warehouse manager, or similar position where I can be a productive liaison between the warehouse and management

Summary

- Four years' experience in military press warehouse
- Hardworking, loyal, ambitious, eager to learn
- Able to view problems in a positive way and propose solutions
- Interested in streamlining operations and improving conditions
- Possess excellent working relations with warehouse staff
- Experienced liaison between workers and management
- Established uniform quantity of books per box at Hilltop, allowing for efficient stacking and shipping, more accurate inventory, and less damage to books
- Installed computer terminal at warehouse for immediate update of inventory

Education

B.A., Liberal Arts, Florida State University, Tallahassee, FL, 1996

Employment History

2000–2004
U.S. Navy, received several promotions in rank

1998–2000
Warehouseman, Hilltop Press, Cocoa Beach, FL

1996–1998
Assistant Foreman, Datalink Computer, Moro, FL

References, including complete military records, available upon request

• ORLANDO B. MARTINEZ

11 Hillcrest Drive • Columbia, SC 29202 • (803) 555-1859
orlando.martinez@xxx.com

• EXPERIENCE

2002 - 2005
Equal Opportunity Program Specialist, U.S. Navy (E-7)
Classification: Chief Petty Officer
Duties: Served as adviser to officers on equal opportunity matters, provided training in nondiscrimination practices, assisted in formulating and revising equal opportunity directives, performed related duties

1999 - 2002
Personnelman, U.S. Navy (E-6)
Classification: Advanced from Personnelman Third Class to Personnelman
  First Class
Duties: Provided a variety of personnel-administration duties

1997 - 1999
Seaman, U.S. Navy (E-3)
Duties: Performed basic seamanship functions

• EDUCATION

B.S. in Political Science, University of South Carolina, 2002
Minor: Sociology

Graduate, Defense Equal Opportunity Training Institute, 1999

Completed Navy Instructor Training Program, 1999

• REFERENCES

Available on request

Chapter 6

Sample Cover Letters

This chapter contains sample cover letters for people pursuing a wide variety of jobs and careers after their military service.

There are many different styles of cover letters in terms of layout, level of formality, and presentation of information. These samples also represent people with varying amounts of education and work experience. Choose one cover letter or borrow elements from several different cover letters to help you construct your own.

CARTER KATZ

474 East Triangle Street

Adrian, MI 49221

(517) 555-2686

carterkatz@xxx.com

July 16, 20—

Nancy Gregg, Human Resources Manager
Harris Corporation
P.O. Box 2929
670 South Mason Street
Indianapolis, IN 46204

Dear Ms. Gregg:

The enclosed resume is submitted in application for the position of Mail Services Manager as announced July 15.

Past supervisors have commented on my high-energy approach to work and life. I'd like to use my substantial experience in mail room management to assist your mail room with the types of duties described in the job announcement. As you will see, the responsibilities I fulfilled while serving in the military were very similar to those expected of this position.

I would be interested in meeting with you in person to discuss the position requirements and how I might address them. I would also be eager to provide letters of recommendation or any other details you might request.

Thank you very much for your consideration. I admire the outstanding image that your company has developed and hope that I can become a part of your organization. You can reach me at any time by calling the number listed. I look forward to hearing from you.

Yours truly,

Carter Katz

Shawna A. Jefferson
238 Heather Avenue
Sioux City, Iowa 51104
(712) 555-0960 Home
(712) 555-7430 Cellular
shawnajefferson@xxx.com

November 29, 20—

Ms. Jenny Mitchell, Attorney at Law
Turner, Smith, Rose, and Mitchell
22 Appleton Building
4003 Smith Plaza
Pierre, South Dakota 57501

Dear Ms. Mitchell:

As you may recall, I spoke with you last year regarding possible employment with your firm following completion of my military duty. Now that my Navy career has concluded, I would like to express my interest in employment with your firm.

Enclosed is a copy of my resume for your perusal. As you will note, I have had considerable experience in a paralegal capacity. It is my hope to build upon my military background by working in a leading law practice such as your own.

I would appreciate the opportunity to talk with you in person to discuss your firm's needs for paralegal assistance and how I might meet them. I would be happy to come to Pierre at any time, either to talk informally or to participate in a formal interview. Please let me know if I can provide any additional information for your review.

I look forward to hearing from you.

Sincerely yours,

Shawna A. Jefferson

Rachel E. Huan
275 Rolling Hills Drive
Toms River, New Jersey 08753
(201) 555-6622 home
(201) 555-8890 cellular phone
rachelhuan@xxx.com

March 6, 20—

George H. King, Owner
Rapid Printing, Inc.
P.O. Box 7112
Morristown, New Jersey 07963-7112

Dear Mr. King:

I am writing to inquire about possible employment with your company. I have seen your advertisements and am aware of the broad range of printing services you provide. I would be very interested in joining your staff should a position become available.

My background in the printing field includes four years' experience with the U.S. Army. Serving as a Printing and Binding Specialist, I performed a wide range of printing services. This includes operating various types of printing equipment while utilizing a teamwork approach in providing excellent service.

I am enclosing a copy of my resume for your review. If you would like additional information, I would be glad to provide it. Please let me know if you would like to meet in person to discuss your employment needs.

Thank you for considering my resume. I hope to hear from you soon.

Sincerely,

Rachel Huan

Lisa M. Henry
532 Monitor Drive
Columbus, OH 43215
(614) 555-3987
lisahenry@xxx.com

August 18, 20—

Charles Metzger, President
Hoffman Enterprises
P.O. Box 344
Cleveland, OH 44102

Dear Mr. Metzger:

Please accept the enclosed resume and samples of my work in application for the position of Staff Photographer with your company. I am responding to the position announcement that appeared in the August 14 edition of the *Plain Dealer*.

I have just concluded a highly successful tour of duty with the U.S. Navy. During this time I specialized in providing a wide variety of photographic services, and my photos received a great deal of acclaim from superior officers and others.

I am highly skilled in both color and black-and-white photography, effective composition, efficient darkroom techniques, and various types of specialized photography. I would be happy to provide additional examples of my work. I would also be willing to take on a sample assignment so that you can judge not only my abilities as a photographer but also my resourcefulness in completing assignments. Of course, I would appreciate an opportunity to meet with you in person and discuss the position more fully.

Please contact me if I can provide additional information. I look forward to the prospect of talking with you.

Yours sincerely,

Lisa M. Henry

Allison Gosney
206 Jeffries Drive
Riverdale, NY 10471
(212) 555-2013
a.gosney@xxx.com

September 12, 20—

Clifford Cox, Personnel Manager
First Flight Airlines
53 Airport Road
Wheeling, WV 26003

Dear Mr. Cox:

Thank you for taking the time to talk with me yesterday about employment possibilities with your airline. Your enthusiasm about First Flight is contagious, and I am highly interested in following up on our conversation.

Enclosed is a copy of my resume. You will see, as we discussed, that I have gained appropriate experience as an Air Passenger Specialist in the United States Air Force. In this capacity I performed a wide range of tasks in providing service for air passengers, and I also completed relevant job training.

I am a self-motivated employee who enjoys working with the public. I have excellent communications skills as well as strong organizational capabilities.

Please review my background and call me at the number listed if you would like to talk further. I would be available for an interview at any time.

Thank you for your consideration.

Sincerely,

Allison Gosney

Lisa Erdman

398 Berger Street
Medford, OR 97501
(503) 555-8007
Lisa-Erdman@xxx.com

January 17, 20—

Mr. Stanley Moore
Ames Construction
604 Dexter Avenue
Seattle, WA 98109

Dear Mr. Moore:

Have you ever wished you could find someone with an old-fashioned work ethic? Someone who knows the job and does it well every day? Past coworkers and supervisors have told me I am that kind of person. Please accept this letter and the enclosed resume in application for the position of Payroll Coordinator that was recently advertised by your company.

My background in payroll work, obtained through military training and experience, has provided me with a firm foundation in performing payroll functions and related business operational tasks. I am experienced in maintaining personnel financial records, processing vouchers for receipt and expenditure of funds, preparing payroll checks, and other key functions.

I would appreciate your review of the enclosed resume. Please let me know if I can become a part of your company's future. I will be glad to meet with you at any time to discuss employment possibilities with your firm.

Your consideration is appreciated.

Sincerely yours,

Lisa Erdman

ROBERTO A. REYES
1378 Orchard Street NE
Santa Fe, NM 87501
(505) 555-4056
robertoreyes@xxx.com

June 1, 20—

Ms. Elizabeth Rowe
Human Resources Manager
Davis Manufacturing
5600 South Main Street
Phoenix, AZ 85009

Dear Ms. Rowe:

I am writing to inquire about employment opportunities with your company. Enclosed is a resume outlining my background and experience.

I am a self-starter with highly developed skills in implementing action plans, meeting goals, and providing leadership for other personnel. As my resume shows, my background includes not only the teamwork required in successful group endeavors but also several years' experience as a Senior Sergeant. In this latter capacity, I work closely with both officers and enlisted personnel, exercising a variety of management and leadership skills.

I would be interested in any position requiring teamwork and a strong work ethic. Please let me know if you have any openings for which I might apply. I will be glad to provide additional details or meet with you for a personal interview.

Thank you for your consideration. I look forward to the prospect of talking with you.

Sincerely,

Roberto A. Reyes

Geoffrey R. Smythe
104 Mount Tabor Road
Elizabeth City, NC 27909
GR.Smythe@xxx.com
(919) 555-2002

February 20, 20—

Alice Wilson, Personnel Manager
Charlotte Memorial Hospital-South
1134 South Highland Street
Charlotte, NC 28220

Dear Ms. Wilson:

I am writing to inquire about employment opportunities with Charlotte Memorial Hospital. Enclosed is a resume outlining my professional experience.

I have an extensive background in the area of medical records. I served for 10 years as a medical records technician in the military, during which time I proved myself a highly reliable and productive worker. I have a strong work ethic and a penchant for accuracy and attention to detail.

My current objective is a position in medical records in a leading facility such as your own. I would be most appreciative if you would consider me for any openings, either now or in the near future.

I would be happy to come to Charlotte for an interview at your convenience. I would also be glad to provide letters of recommendation or other information. Thank you for your consideration. I hope to hear from you soon.

Sincerely yours,

Geoffrey R. Smythe

SHARON L. DUARTE

760 Hunters Mill Road

Helena, AR 72342

(501) 555-2624

s.duarte@xxx.com

April 1, 20—

Mr. Randolph Givens
Vice President
Allied Manufacturing, Inc.
Box 45447
St. Louis, MO 63123

Dear Mr. Givens:

This letter and the enclosed resume are submitted in the event that you may have a position vacancy in your personnel department.

I have a strong background in human resources management through my recent service in the United States Coast Guard. Over the past 15 years, I have specialized in performing comprehensive duties in personnel administration and related management. During this time, I have proved myself to be a diligent and resourceful worker.

Should a position be open now or in the near future, I hope you will consider me. My resume provides basic details regarding my background and experience; if additional information is needed, please contact me by phone or e-mail. I would be glad to meet with you in person at your convenience.

Thank you for considering my application. I would appreciate hearing from you.

Yours truly,

Sharon Duarte

LINDA DIAZ DAVIS

708 Carson Road
Morganton, NC 28655
(704) 555-3795 Home
(704) 555-0990 Cellular
Linda-Davis@xxx.com

October 14, 20—

Mr. Wayne Burris
Director of Personnel
Ace Security Services
21 Jordan Avenue
Athens, GA 30603

Dear Mr. Burris,

I enjoyed our telephone conversation yesterday. Thank you for taking the time to speak with me. As we discussed, my background as a Marine security guard could prove a significant asset should I join your company. I believe I would bring a fresh perspective to your operations and could help in your quest to make Ace an even more effective company.

I was especially interested to learn of your plans to expand your business internationally. My language skills and international experience should prove helpful in this regard.

The enclosed resume provides important details about my background. After you have reviewed it, please let me know if you would like to discuss present or future needs of your company and how I might meet them.

Yours truly,

Linda Diaz Davis

Angela Caruso   1501 Welisford Street
Minneapolis, MN 55455
(612) 555-1373
angela.caruso@xxx.com

July 11, 2—

Madison Life, Incorporated
415 Orleans Street
Chicago, IL 60610

Dear Personnel Manager:

I understand that your firm employs a number of word-processing special-ists, administrative assistants, and other clerical and administrative sup-port personnel. I specialized in such functions while serving in the United States Marine Corps. Now that my military service has concluded, I would like to apply my skills and experience to the corporate world.

Enclosed is a copy of my resume. As you will see, I have a broad range of experience in providing office support services. I am a team player with excel-lent technical skills, outstanding communication capabilities, and the capac-ity to carry a heavy workload.

I would be most interested in discussing with you any opportunities for employment with your firm. Please contact me if you would like additional information.

Thank you for your consideration.

Sincerely,

Angela Caruso

COLLEEN QUINN

3104 Linden Court • Bradford, MA 01830
Home: (508) 555-9576 • Cellular: (508) 555-0909
E-mail: cquinn@xxx.com

December 6, 20—

Thomas Gaines
General Manager
Electronic Systems Technology, Inc.
210 Northview Drive
Amarillo, TX 79178

Dear Mr. Gaines:

Thank you for talking with me today. I enjoyed our telephone conversation. As you requested, I am enclosing a copy of my resume. This will provide you with specific details regarding my experience, training, and overall qualifications.

You will see that I have a great deal of experience in servicing and repairing computer equipment, with special emphasis on advanced communications systems. My Army background has prepared me to work with a wide range of equipment, and I have proved to be a reliable, conscientious, and highly productive technician.

I would appreciate the opportunity to meet with you in person to discuss your company's needs for qualified technicians, as well as my capabilities for fulfilling them. Now that my military service has concluded, I am eager to take on a challenging position in the private sector. I will certainly appreciate being considered for any openings that your firm might have.

Thank you again for taking the time to talk with me. I look forward to hearing from you.

Sincerely,

Colleen Quinn

JASON RASKIN

1005 University Blvd.
Fort Collins, CO 80523
(303) 555-6922
jasonraskin@xxx.com

August 21, 20—

William Anderson, President
Anderson Ford, Inc.
Box 2198
Boulder, CO 80301-2198

Dear Mr. Anderson:

I understand that your dealership operates a substantial auto body repair business along with the other aspects of selling and repairing automobiles. I am an experienced specialist in auto body repair and as such would like to offer my services should a position become available.

Enclosed is a copy of my resume. You will see that I have nearly 10 years' experience in performing a variety of tasks related to auto body repair. Most of this experience came as a result of my military service, where I performed with excellence and received very positive evaluations from my superiors.

If a position opens with your company, I would appreciate being considered. I would be happy to provide additional information by mail or telephone or to come for an interview.

Thank you for any consideration you might give me regarding possible employment. I look forward to talking with you.

Sincerely,

Jason Raskin

STUART PURDY JR.

Route 4, Box 189 • Winfield, KS 67156
(316) 555-0370 home • (316) 555-9676 cellular
stuartpurdy@xxx.com

May 1, 20—

Allison P. Smith, Vice President for Marketing
Bell's of Topeka
Topeka, KS 66603

Dear Ms. Smith:

As an individual eager to pursue a career in sales and marketing, I am submitting the enclosed resume for your review. I have a strong orientation toward the marketing function and would appreciate being considered as an addition to your staff.

My background includes both retail sales and extensive experience as a recruiter for the U.S. Army. In the latter capacity, I was fortunate to gain invaluable background in human relations, communication skills, time management, self-motivation, and other attributes necessary for successful marketing.

I am a hard worker who is willing to learn new skills and techniques. My positive attitude and emphasis on teamwork would be valuable assets for your organization. I would be very grateful for the chance to talk with you and further explore your company's needs. Please call me and let me know if we might arrange to meet.

Thank you for your consideration.

Sincerely,

Stuart Purdy Jr.

• ORLANDO B. MARTINEZ

11 Hillcrest Drive • Columbia, SC 29202 • (803) 555-1859
orlando.martinez@xxx.com

March 31, 20—

Roberta Shumate, Director of Personnel Services
University of South Carolina
P.O. Box 1122
Columbia, SC 29202

Dear Ms. Shumate:

I enjoyed talking with you yesterday about the affirmative action program officer's position that was advertised in *The State*. Please let me reiterate my interest in the position.

Enclosed for your review is a copy of my resume. You will note that I have had significant experience in promoting affirmative action and conducting related personnel functions. My military experience has provided me a wealth of understanding in this area and given me the chance to work and live with a diverse group of people. I believe I would do very well in the university setting and would be of service to others in the collegiate climate.

After studying the description for the position at your institution and discussing some of the details with you, I believe that my background provides a solid match with your expressed needs. I would be happy to amplify on my qualifications and interests through a personal interview.

If you would like to discuss this matter, please contact me by e-mail or telephone. I look forward to hearing from you.

Sincerely,

Orlando Martinez

✚ Denise Jackson-Smith

906 Fair Meadow Street
Dayton, OH 45469
(513) 555-9765
denise.jacksonsmith@xxx.com

October 4, 20—

Douglas Sharpson
Medquip, Inc.
1033 Payton Avenue, South
Columbus, OH 43215

Dear Mr. Sharpson:

Would you like to be able to truly rely on your newest service technician, from day one? I am a quick learner, highly responsible, and a person who does things right the first time. As you can see from the three letters of recommendation requested by your advertisement in *The Post,* I have been highly praised by my coworkers and superiors alike.

A period of seven years in the military spent repairing, maintaining, and servicing medical equipment under all kinds of challenging field conditions has given me the confidence to state that I am highly qualified to join your team. My work with diverse individuals has given me the background needed to be a valuable team player.

Your company has been recommended to me by a number of friends who work in medical technology. I believe Medquip is a company that could give me the chance to build on my solid military background while contributing my unique skills to a high-tech, high-service team.

I would be happy to provide more details or to come meet with you at your convenience. Thank you for your consideration. I look forward to hearing from you.

Yours truly,

Denise Jackson-Smith

HARRISON TILLMAN

420 Reagan Road
Fort Smith, AR 72913
(501) 555-0409
harrisontillman@xxx.com

November 13, 20—

Mr. Andrew Davis
Division Manager
Superior Drug Stores
212 Imperial Place
Dallas, TX 75265

Dear Mr. Davis:

Enclosed is my resume for your consideration. I am interested in suitable openings in your chain of stores in the states of Arkansas, Texas, or New Mexico.

My Army training and work assignments as an assistant to pharmacists will make me a valuable addition to your operation. A position as pharmacy technician, assistant store manager, or distribution support staff member would be appropriate to my skills and background.

I have a strong work ethic that will allow me to make a significant contribution to your company. Although I am currently enrolled as a full-time student, I am available for employment at the completion of the current semester. In addition, I would be happy to relocate.

Please let me know if you would like more information about my qualifications. I hope you will consider me for any appropriate position openings, and I look forward to hearing from you soon.

Sincerely yours,

Harrison Tillman